A Journey Through Darkness

A Story of Inspiration

A Journey
Through Darkness

A Story of Inspiration

By Margareth Maganga

MKUKI NA NYOTA
DAR-ES-SALAAM

PUBLISHED BY
Mkuki na Nyota Publishers Ltd
Nyerere Road, Quality Plaza Building
P. O. Box 4246
Dar es Salaam, Tanzania
www.mkukinanyota.com
publish@mkukinanyota.com

© Margareth Maganga, 2012

ISBN 978 9987 08 221 6

Contents

Dedicated to my family –
Dad, Mum, Evarist, Raphael and Lucky Maganga

Even if I go through the deepest darkness, I will not be afraid, LORD, for you are with me. Your shepherd's rod and staff protect me.

Psalms 23:4

FOREWORD

This is the true story of Margareth Maganga. Maggy, as she is commonly known confronted a situation until then unknown to most of us lay people, and even among very learned medical professionals.

Maggy, went to bed a happy and healthy girl one night and, woke up the following morning, totally blind. What followed is well narrated in this book. Prayers were said to God and the gods. Friends and relations wept, struggled to undo the emerged reality. For her part, Maggy at first did not believe what had happened to her. Why it happened, and why her? What next? Despair or courage-she opted for the latter.

This book, therefore narrates Maggy's experience with unexpected blindness. This is the true account of her struggle to never lose hope, and of the support she received from her parents and well–wishers.

Eventually, and with a strong hope in God's grace, Maggy managed to recover part of her eyesight. She came to the conclusion that her past experience notwithstanding, she would proceed with her long-held ambition to study, Law. While writing this book she pursues her law degree at the University of Leeds, and intends to practice law to help those in need of legal services but who cannot afford to engage lawyers or fight for their rights.

As you go through this book, no doubt, one lesson emerges: never lose hope. Trust in God. However you may be handicapped, you have a role to play in ameliorating the lives of the majority, especially those who are desperately struggling for survival. It is our duty,; all of us-including you who intends to read this book now – to make the world a better place for all God's creatures rich and poor, healthy and sick. Go ahead, read this book and live the lessons you derive from Maggy's experience.

Justice Dr. Steven Bwana, J.A.
Court of Appeal of Tanzania

ACKNOWLEDGEMENTS

Glory be to God, for He never abandoned me – even when it was darkness all around me and fears within.

So much love and thanks to my father, Paschal Maganga, for his tireless dedication to pay all my medical bills and for the love, prayers and encouragement. For reassuring me of his endless love and giving me hope when my faith had quivered. My mother, Jane Paschal, for being my best friend, and lending me a listening ear throughout all the rough and unexplainable moments. Thank you so much also for encouraging me to write this book in order to inspire people. No one has ever given, me more love and valuable support than you. Were it not for you, I doubt if I would have made it this far. I love you infinitely.

A special thanks to my brothers, Evarist for his confidence in the production of this book, inspiration and tenacity, and Raphael for getting all his friends all over the world to keep me in their prayers, and Lucky for using my testimony to candidates as an encouragement to believe in the power of prayer. To the three of you, I have always loved you, still do and always will. To my cousins Agnes and Aneth, thank you for always being there to provide a shoulder to lean on. Without forgetting Exaud (Chaya) Thomas for being my 'personal secretary' and helping me keep in touch with all my friends while in hospital.

Big thanks to my aunt, Anna Mukami, for her support and great hospitality while in Washington DC and my uncle, Peter Maganga, for accommodating us during our entire stay in Massachusetts and encouraging his friends to pay us visits during that period. My sincerest gratitude to the entire community of Tanzanians and Kenyans living in Massachusetts, whose support and spirit of togetherness made us feel welcome in their community, especially Virginia Mugure, Lydia, Jamal Rajin, Geliga, Casmille, Lindiwe Hume and Yvonne Mugure, just to mention a few.

Many thanks to Justice Dr. S.J. Bwana of the Court of Appeal of Tanzania, for always encouraging me to study Law, and his unfailing support throughout my sickness together with his beloved family (especially Tina); and the entire family of Mrs. Loyce Nyalali; Mrs. Norah Rusobya, James Andrew Bwana; Lucas Mashauri; Perusy Nyakila; Mr. & Mrs. Obeto; Mrs. Angelina Manko; Mrs. Judith Joshua; Adventina Maganga Mrs. Nellie Keya; Hon. S. Kalonzo Musyoka, the Vice President of Kenya; B.K. Sikudhan, for their support, advice, generosity and regular visits during and after my hospitalization.

Thanks to Kenneth Limen, for all his support, suggestions, motivation, encouragement, and friendship to my family, especially during the time of my ordeal and even after.

Thanks to the entire community of the Kenya High School, particularly my best friends, Georgina Amayo, Charlene Migwe and Betsy Keya, for their constant love, encouragement and true friendship, and my teacher, Miss Leah Tuimur for being my first point of contact at the school and for her support and prayers.

Thanks to my friends at the University of Leeds; Trish Rodrigues, Hira Jamal, Hamad Al-Musfir, Farhan Shafee, Mark Odhiambo, Tanveer Mansur, Omair Jamal and Azy Aziz for assisting me in adapting to my new lifestyle when I needed it most. And for your constant love and support.

Thanks to my tutor Dr. Tom Hawes for editing the manuscript and always encouraging me to achieve my goals in school. Many thanks also to Dr. Anna Mdee for her positive feedback after going through the manuscript.

Many thanks to Pr. Sando, Pr. Sinda, Pr. Ngusa and Pr. Machage for your dedicated prayers; Mary Obunde for all your help while in Taiwan; the Iringo SDA Church, for your songs of encouragement, and Leeds SDA Church, for welcoming me into your fellowship family.

Many thanks to the management and staff of Comprehensive Community Based Rehabilitation in Tanzania, especially Dr. Richard Bowman for his devotion in the fight against blindness; UMass Memorial Medical Centre, especially Dr. Julie Pilitsis for using her gifted hands in trying to restore my vision; and Leeds

University Transcription Centre for providing me with reading and learning materials to help me work independently and achieve my full potential.

And, finally, to all those who have not been mentioned, but have in so many ways helped me to be where I am right now, thank you ever so much.

INTRODUCTION

Many of us may live our lives without ever stopping to think 'What if I couldn't see?' We hardly ever ask ourselves this question because, to say the least, we take our eyes for granted.

Like most people, I had never thought about it until January 11, 2008. My mother came to wake me up that Friday morning and asked me what I was still doing in bed and confidently I replied, "Because it is still dark outside, Mum." In her astonishment she told me it was 8am and the sun was shining bright (a typical African morning!). I rubbed my eyes, opened them wider but it was still dark. I yelled out, "I can't see! I can't see!" I wept day in, day out, but the distress and its pain became mute with time. Darkness – unforgiving, uncomfortable, endless – was something that played on and caused a nuisance to my life of just nineteen years. Upon seeking treatment, I was diagnosed with pseudotumor celebri – a rare disorder of unknown etiology found predominantly in obese women of childbearing age caused by chronically elevated intracranial pressure in the brain. It was bizarre, especially for my family and friends, but for me, that was the beginning of a long journey through a forest of darkness, where the bright full moon and the stars had been extinguished; was my world dark and uncertain.

I started writing "A journey through darkness" in March 2008, after being inspired by Richard Moore, founder and director of "Children in Crossfire." Richard's work is all the more remarkable given that he himself was blinded at the age of ten after a rubber bullet was fired at point blank range into his face. In some, such an event might have left bitterness, but in Richard, it left a desire to help others. Imagining myself to have grown up beautifully, then suddenly finding myself visually impaired and worse, made me believe that I could also help others by writing a book. The idea was that £1 from every copy sold would be donated to support education for the visually challenged primary school students as they gain entry into secondary schools in East Africa, giving them the best possible chance of an independent future. The book is also to inspire you, dear reader and to give hope to those with none left. It is to reveal God's constant love and mercy towards His people – believers and non-believers.

I started getting up in the wee hours, sitting by my dressing table, trying to remember as much as I could, then putting my thoughts down in a genuine bonded leather flex journal. The writing process was a huge obstacle as my eyes were completely out of my immediate line of vision, which made me drop the writing for a while until I enrolled at the University of Leeds in September 2008. There I found Leeds University Transcription Centre, which provided me with essential visual aids for my reading and learning.

My writing picked up speed. Nearly every night after returning from university, I sat by my study desk writing a sentence or two. Months went by, but I kept to my routine until I finally completed the writing in December 2009. I kept the manuscript in a safe place, waiting for the right moment for it to be born. That came in January 11, 2010, exactly two years after the original incident, when my brother, Evarist was convinced I should give him the manuscript to type it out and give it to his friend, who he thought could help me edit it for publication. That started the process that ends with the book you hold in your hands.

The story I have written here is an honest account of a particularly trying moment of my life and the dialogue is an approximation of what was actually said to me. Some of the characters that appear are various people I have known, and some events appear out of exact chronology. Therefore, with the exception of my family, the names of most of people have been changed out of respect for their privacy.

Nonetheless, it is to my family that I dedicate this book. I hope you get as much pleasure and inspiration out of reading about them and that every page brings you closer to understanding the love and respect I feel for them.

Part One

It was a sparkling Saturday, January 5, 2008, the sun out in full force, the sky a limpid blue in the beautiful city of Taipei, Taiwan. It was the final day of the World Youth Conference for Adventist Youth. Young people from across oceans and continents convened for the conference. From Tanzania, we were a delegation of approximately thirty-eight. To us, that was a large number but not as large as the South Koreans, who numbered hundreds. As the day wore on, I started feeling feverish, and then there was muscle pain growing bit by bit around my neck. Not wanting to look unwell, I ignored the pain and tried to keep an outward façade of cheerfulness. Of course I was deceiving no one but myself as I was bleeding inside and this intensified pain became unbearable at noon. Even the constant flow of tears could not wash it away. I had asked for some pain killers which only soothed the pain for a while.

The events of the day came to a finale at around 9pm. As we fumbled around looking for buses, others exchanged contacts, recalling how that one week had been a great time for many youths. I entered my bus not interested in getting any form of contacts (pause there; this is Maggie the extrovert we are talking about!) Whenever I meet new people I always make sure I leave with enough contacts to make me buy a new phone book. My friends in high school can testify to that. I didn't believe what was happening to me this time. The fever had increased, my head was throbbing, and my neck was experiencing the most excruciating pain I have ever had. In the bus I couldn't get a comfortable position on my seat to rest my head. The journey from the conference centre to the hostel was almost one hour but it felt like an eternity.

When we finally reached the hostel I got out of the bus still feeling weak. Dorcas, also from Tanzania, was there to help me when I almost fell to the ground after losing my balance. She asked me what was wrong. This time, I couldn't lie that I was well while I wasn't. I wept in frustration as I told her of the headache that I had. At that particular moment I felt so bad that I wished I had

1

not lived, but it was a sort of migraine that assured me I would continue to suffer but not die. She called Mary, my roommate and together they helped me to my room. Dorcas volunteered to give me a neck massage, which sadly didn't help. I took another pain killer but that was no good either.

As my condition worsened, one of my friends alerted our youth leaders, who had accompanied us to the conference. I was lying on my back on my bed when in a short time my room flocked with well wishers. Some of the friends I had made during the week came too. After a short discussion the leaders decided that I should be rushed to the hospital. Perhaps, that is why they say, 'the older the wiser,' since the thought had not crossed my mind the entire time. The hostel staff called for a taxi as I trailed down to the lobby. One of the friends I had made, Dean, an Australian, was shocked to see me in that state because during the day he had seen me full of life. He wanted to accompany me to the hospital but the taxi couldn't take all of us.

I went with Mary and one other hostel staff member. The ride to the hospital seemed to take forever. When we arrived the doctor questioned me about my symptoms. I tried explaining as much as I could. They drew some blood for lab tests. To calm my nerves, I was given a shot of some pain medicine, which actually helped to the. extent that I managed to get some sleep on Mary's shoulder. She took out her phone and made a call to my parents to inform them of my condition. From their conversation, I could tell that my parents were overwhelmed with feelings of fear and great concern since Mary kept reassuring them that everything was under control.

When the results from the lab came out, the doctor told me that I was chronically anemic. I had never known that before. He gave us two options: either to have a blood transfusion or tablets to keep me going until the time I arrived home because we were leaving for Dar-es-Salaam, that very Sunday, January 6, at around 4pm. After receiving a dose of glucose I was transferred to another hospital. There I was also asked similar questions and more tests were carried out. The results came out, and coincided with the previous ones. So the doctor gave me a few tablets and at dawn the following day we headed back to the hostel.

When I arrived I went straight to bed as Mary helped me pack my suitcase and that of my younger brother, Lucky. He hadn't known I had gone to the hospital. But, I could tell he was building up a close understanding of what was going on as he put on a sensitive and empathetic look. I don't know for how long I slept but I woke up when Michael, one of my friends from Zambia came to visit me. He hadn't known either that I had spent my night at the hospital. He was shocked, disturbed, you name it. He brought me a rose flower, a letter with sweet encouraging words and then he prayed with me. He soon left since he had to catch an earlier flight than mine. The first friend I made in Taiwan was the Australian Youth Leader Mr. Nick Ross, a very friendly person. He came into the room I shared with Mary to find out how I was doing as he was also leaving, which made me slightly emotional for he had portrayed such a fatherly and friendly figure throughout the conference. Mary had taught him to greet in Swahili since he was so intrigued by the language. When he finally said goodbye I could not help but shed a few tears.

At 2pm our bus was leaving for the airport. That was when I knew I wouldn't see most of the friends I had made again, and parting with them was such sweet sorrow. The whole journey to the airport I was sobbing inconsolably and so was Mary. Lucky just looked, and at some point jeered at me, an indirect indication that the parting with friends was an affecting scene, but poignant grief could not endure forever. That is Lucky, he always seems to take things so lightly, or maybe it is I who am too emotional. After checking in at the airport, I finally made my mind up to leave my poignant anxiety and Taipei behind. There was a long journey ahead of us and I wouldn't want to get sick in mid-air. Throughout the whole journey from Taipei to Dar-es-Salam via Hong Kong and Doha – I tried to think of only the good times I had had at the conference. The journey was long but finally we arrived in Dar-es-Salaam at around 1pm on Monday, January 7.

Dar-es-Salaam, Tanzania's economic capital is usually hot for most of the year, blazing and humid. At the airport we bid long farewells to each other as we exchanged contacts, before going our separate ways. Lucky and I had to rush for our connecting flight to Mwanza, a city in northwest Tanzania and a southern port of Lake Victoria; Africa's largest freshwater lake. We made our flight that took approximately one hour and ten minutes. As soon as the plane was in the air, I felt my face and neck get hot, then a painful throb in the head. I expected some kind of relief when we commenced the descent, but this was not to be. As we touched down, my headache intensified. My cousin, Aneth, had come to pick us up along with Godfrey, the family driver. We had another long journey from Mwanza to Musoma, my beautiful but relatively small hometown which was not less than three hours' drive away.

As we made our journey, inside the car I couldn't find a comfortable position to rest my head on as I felt a dull persistent neck pain. For a moment, I could not either feel the pain and then in a heartbeat or two, a fresh somatic sensation of acute discomfort came flooding through me, shaking me to my core as I stifled a cry of agony. Everyone in the car looked at me with tender compassion at my distress. I prayed amidst my cries for God to at least give me peace as I fell asleep and woke up when we had reached home. Everyone at home could not conceal their excitement when they saw us back, especially my parents, my elder brother, Raphael and my other cousins. The pain momentarily eased away; laughter, relief and joy dominated.

The following day, Tuesday, January 8, I experienced pain like never before. My head kept pounding as if a gong had been implanted in the brain, and my neck felt like it was being pulled apart as in a tug-of-war. I stayed in my room almost the entire day, not wanting to see anyone at all. In the evening, I took some more analgesic drugs that only relieved me for a while. During the night,

I clenched my teeth, I tossed and turned and kicked my bedding away. When I couldn't take it anymore, I got up and knocked at my parents' room. Mum opened the door, keenly waiting for me to tell her about my predicament. I explained to her that I couldn't sleep, my voice sounding frail with gloomy distress. Mum wished she could bear my pain as she held me close in her arms. She handed me a pill in a little cup.

"You'll feel better after you get some sleep," she said.

I nodded and said, "Good night, Mum," feeling dismissed.

"Good night, sweetheart," she said, with her favourite term of endearment.

At dawn I prepared myself to go to the hospital. Some of my friends and relatives stopped me on the way to see how I was doing. This is not strange since we live in a small town, and everyone seems to know each other. At the hospital it seemed like forever before I was attended to, typical of the healthcare system at home, nevertheless I couldn't complain for there were signs of doctors in the hospital so eventually I would get a consultation. When the doctor read the diagnosis reports that I was given in Taiwan, he wanted some more tests done. To my shock and disbelief, the hospital equipment had broken down and no one had reported the matter to the authorities. Having no other alternative, the doctor referred me to the Muhimbili National Hospital in Dar-es-salaam. With sadness and displeasure, I returned home. At home, I lost my appetite for everything, even as Mum prepared her gourmet dishes, my stomach could not take it, but they forced some down my throat, having not succeeded in begging to eat on my own. Later in the day I threw up a lot. I regained my appetite soon after and ravenously ate the food before taking a nap.

In Africa, a child is for the community, they say. So friends, relatives and neighbours dropped by our house to find out how I was doing. They were all filled with pity as they watched me on my bed writhe in pain. The thick unpleasant muck of bleakness was nothing new to me, I had battled with it in some way since Taiwan.

They wished me a quick recovery and good health. After all the visitors had left, I took a nap for a while before joining the rest of the family in the sitting room, as Aneth helped me pack my clothes for the trip to Dar-es-Salaam the very next day.

On Thursday, January 10, 2008, I woke up with no pain but kept seeing flashes here and there, hence I could not keep them open. Early in the morning we started our journey to Dar-es-Salaam (Dar). We drove till Mwanza and then took a plane to Dar. As we took off from Mwanza Dad, Mum and I, did not know what lay ahead of us. Dad and I dozed off as soon as our plane took off while Mum read her bible because she has difficulty sleeping when travelling. Dad and I on the other hand, we normally sleep as soon as we comfortably settle into our seats be it in a bus, plane or car. In one hour we were landing at the Mwl. Julius Nyerere Airport. Dar at that time of the year was annoyingly hot and humid. I felt like I was almost out of breath. Then, Dad and I started sweating profusely so we had to keep dabbing our foreheads every few minutes. Since my eyes were still flashing about, I was not given any luggage to carry lest I fall with it. We took a taxi to one of the hotels in the city and checked in before heading to the hospital. I had never been to Muhimbili but I had heard a lot about it.

One significant thing about the hospitals at home is the distinct and irritating smell of medicine and detergent from a long way off. You know where a hospital is by the odour of drugs. When we got to the hospital we were directed out and about the hospital. The first physician who attended to me after hearing how I was feeling signed me up for an admission. I don't recall ever being admitted before but Mum says when I was young, the hospital was almost my second home! Dad suggested we go for lunch first and then go back to the hospital for the admission. Splendid idea for I was already hungry. One could tell by the way my lips were dry. All this time I was holding Mum's hand because I couldn't open my eyes to the sun as it really affected them and I kept seeing flashes of bright lights everywhere.

After a heavy meal we headed back to the hospital. We were escorted to the ward in which I was supposed to be admitted. People were crowded outside. The stench of medicines, detergents and other strong chemicals filled the air, making it almost unbearable for one to breathe in. It wasn't a place that anyone would like to stay in. On entering, I almost fainted at the sight of the ward. There were so many patients, even on the floor! People were groaning and moaning in pain. For a moment I felt I wasn't sick at all and I could go back home because people had bigger problems than mine. One particular lady made my eyes watery as she was nothing but a bag of bones. She stretched out her bony and feeble hands and begged for anyone to feel pity on her and give her something to eat. Her hair seemed to have fallen out, her collar bones sticking out like one who had gone without food and water for months. She wore clothes that had seen better days. Another lady lying on a mattress on the floor was reading her Bible. She knew where to look for help during difficult times. We later learned that she had a heart condition. There was another one who was covered from head to toe with a white bed sheet. You needed not to be told that she had left for her heavenly abode.

My eyes kept peering into the room although still with difficulty. I told my parents that I wasn't going to be admitted for I felt I would get worse. Finally the doctor came to attend to me. She was a young lady, looking professional in her white lab coat and had put on a pair of round rimmed glasses. She began examining me by questioning me incessantly. For a split moment I thought I was in the dock in court and she a ruthless prosecutor for she wanted me to narrate everything without leaving out the minutest detail. She was interrogating me! She wrote down that I should have some tests done the very next day. We asked for a discharge and she granted us one. As the cross examination, if I may call it that, was going on, one of my uncles-Andrew an attorney at law-came together with his lovely wife, aunt Lucy as they had heard of our visit to Dar and had come to see us. Aunt Lucy, very charming and friendly, was with Mum and I as Dad was with Uncle Andrew outside. As we waited for the doctor to officially discharge me, we kept talking about the condition of the ward, my sickness and other things that women do talk about. We left shortly after and headed back to the hotel. I had to congratulate my uncle on choosing such a beautiful gem of a wife as I had never met her before. Little did I know that it would be the last I saw of them for several months-not because they would be away but because of what would happen the very next day.

Part Two

Some people make jokes like, "Imagine some guy went to sleep and woke up dead!" Ha! That is definitely impossible, but this is not. I went to bed in my normal state, but I woke up not seeing the blessed light of day. Mum came to wake me up to go to the hospital on that fateful Friday, January 11, 2008. I woke up and it was dark, and I was puzzled at why Mum was knocking at my door that early. Hardly had I opened the door and when Mum asked me why I was still sleeping. I groaned as I told her that it was still dark outside. She told me it was 8am, clearly not amused thinking it was one of my excuses to stay in bed a bit longer.

"What! Then how come all I can see is darkness?" I asked.

"Maggie, stop joking. What do you mean it is dark? Look out the window." She asked to her astonishment.

"Mum, I am serious, I can't see anything." I screamed in disbelief, while darting my eyes all round the room, hoping I was dreaming.

Mum then realized I was serious as she saw me prodding for the wall and then the bed to look for my things to go to the shower. At this time tears were rolling down my cheeks uncontrollably. Mum helped me get ready then she went off to tell Dad the devastating news. No news is good news, so they say. Soon we were going to the restaurant for breakfast as Mum was holding my hand. I had gone blind! I was blind! I choked with tears as I thought this. I thought that if I closed my eyes and opened them suddenly I would see again but to no avail. I was blind. I couldn't even take my breakfast well. No one did. Even the waiters and waitresses in the hotel were shocked since they had seen me the previous day and I had been fine. From the way Mum talked I could tell she was crying, although very silently.

We got to the hospital confused. The doctor had ordered many tests to be done, x-rays ECG, blood test and many others. I waited for Dad to register me as I sat outside on a bench crying. I kept wondering what would become of me now that I was blind. I could not even say the word out loud. It was too painful, I did not want to accept it, I just couldn't.

"It cannot be! No! I am not blind! This can't be real," I tried to reassure myself. But oh how real it was!

I thought of how I wouldn't go to regular schools or wouldn't see the faces of my parents, brothers, relatives and friends. I wouldn't read or write normally. No TV or computers. No movies, no emails, no texting. The more I thought, the more I cried. I closed my eyes so that it wouldn't hurt me that I could actually not see. I shuddered at the thought of having to learn Braille! I cried to God and asked Him never-ending questions.

My mind went round and round with the same barrage of questions, like a persistent police interrogation. 'Why' is a small word but with a big question mark. Why God? Why? I'm only nineteen, my life is actually starting. God I have just finished my high school and my results are not even out. Life is a natural healing process, we are told. Life certainly takes unexplained twists and turns and this is one of them!

I cried even more. Mum tried comforting me even though she was finding it hard to comfort me while she also didn't have any answers. I would stop crying for a while then start all over again. I could hear people talking, minding their own business. Kids were crying, I guess they were afraid of the jabs they were getting. Other kids were running around playing. I wondered if they could be in my shoes how they would be. I could hear doctors and nurses going off in different directions, phones ringing from different corners, the dragging of feet. I could hear all this but could not see. I cried even more. What I felt at that moment only God and I know. It is not something one can explain easily. How does one explain being able to see one day and not able to see the next? It was always easy to wake up every morning and behold the new day with the slightest of ease without ever thinking that one day it would be snatched from me overnight.

Soon Dad came and took us to the different rooms for the tests to be carried out. Even the doctors gasped when they saw me being guided into the room. They asked what had happened. I was too emotional to say anything so Mum and Dad made all the explanations. The doctors were encouraging. They told me to believe in the healing power of God. One doctor was particularly helpful, she advised us to drop all the other tests and head off to the eye specialists. Up until that moment we had not thought of rushing straight to them. We had been too confused, we did not know where to start so we had opted to go ahead with my scheduled appointments. Thinking of it now, I wonder why we hadn't even rushed out of the hotel and into the eye specialists' office demanding answers for my newly discovered predicament.

Mum and I waited outside as Dad struggled through the crowd to get help. We were called in and I was taken to an optician. After asking me to read some letters which I could not see completely, he said that the problem was beyond him and so he advised us to see the ophthalmologists themselves. We entered another room. I could hear babies crying, mothers explaining, doctors instructing, and the door opening and closing every few minutes. My mother helped me to sit down and before they did anything else, Mum and Dad were asked to leave the room. One female doctor attended to me. I later learned that she was called Dr. Mataka. She asked me to open my eyes wide as she examined them. She called three of her colleagues to come and examine me as well. The way they talked indicated the seriousness of the problem. They said things like, 'the optic disc looks serrated'; 'there is swelling in the eyes, it may be papilloedema', and so on, and so many other technical terms. Hearing this made me cry even more. My body shook, my face shrunk, my stomach knotted, I was in despair.

They called my parents back in and explained to them. Dr. Mataka advised them to take me to the Muhimbili Orthopedic Institute, MOI, for immediate scans. She believed the problem leaned more towards the neurological department. MOI isn't far from the main hospital so we just walked under the scorching sun. We met the doctor who had attended to me the previous time in the ward. She was shocked beyond words when she learnt of what had befallen me. In MOI, we sat and waited for the specialist who had gone for a lunch break. As I waited, the nurses kept asking me what had happened. They did not know that I was not in a mood to talk but I could not be rude since these were the same people who would attend to me. I explained to them briefly. They pitied me, saying I was so young and beautiful and did not deserve to go through what I was going through. (Tarry awhile there… who said only the old and the ugly deserve to get sick?)

One of them told me of a lady preacher who performed healing miracles. They asked me if I would mind them taking me to her. Politely I told them that it was okay if they just prayed for me without necessarily taking me there. I am a strong believer in God so I don't dismiss people who offer their prayers for me. However, at this point I did not want to be made a public spectacle. In any case, I was still coming to terms with the reality myself. After what seemed like an eternity, the doctor finally came and requested for me to have a Computerized Tomography (CT) scan of the brain. We were given directions to the radiology department and headed there anxiously. My cousin, Agnes had been called and been given the horrible news. She came after school and met me just before going for the scan. She had brought along a friend from school. She couldn't believe it as she had seen me briefly at the Mwl. Julius Nyerere airport after my Taiwan trip. I went for the scan, Agnes holding my hand as we passed through different corridors in search of the room. She held me close, making sure I did not walk into people or vice versa. Mum and Dad walked in front of us, leading the way. When we got to the room, it seemed poorly ventilated, stuffy and humid. I was sweating a lot and kept wiping my brow. It was my first time to have a CT scan though I had had an MRI (Magnetic Resonance Imaging) scan before. After about twenty minutes we were done and the specialist said we should wait for the results for some time so we went back to MOI and waited.

My cousin didn't stay long afterwards but promised to come back the next day. I really pitied Dad for he was moving up and down, in and out of the hospital in that sweltering heat. Although I could not see him, I knew he was sweating a lot, that's what the Dar weather does to him. It was not surprising that he was struggling to make sure I got all the medical attention I needed. It reminded me of how he would always go out of his way to make sure we had a home and went to school on time with everything we needed. He has always been hard working and has instilled the same discipline in my brothers and I. When he saw me cry he would comfort me and tell me all would be well if I just trusted God, that He would heal me. Dad is a God-fearing man who is never ashamed to proclaim God's grace, another quality I have learnt from him and Mum.

When the results came out the doctor studied the pictures and complained that the radiologist had not taken the correct tests. He therefore, couldn't diagnose any problem from those scans and said I needed to have others taken. It was already late Friday, thus most offices including the Radiology department were closed. The neurologist told us that we had to get an admission but we rejected the idea of being admitted to Muhimbili. After much thinking he told us of a private doctor's plaza in which most of the doctors from Muhimbili held clinical sessions. We then left to seek admission at Hope Hospital. I tried to look out of the window to at least catch a glimpse of the unfamiliar territory but it was all pitch black outside, with the noise of whooshing cars and honking here and there. On arrival we were lucky enough to find a vacancy. I could neither see the shape nor the colour of the building. To my surprise it did not even possess the distinct odour of medicine and detergent. I could hear wheelchairs being driven past me and a periodic call for a patient to go and see a doctor or report to the reception desk wherever it was. I had been sitting in the waiting area with Mum as Dad dealt with all the registration. On completion, I was wheeled up to my room, not knowing I would spend the next few weeks there.

I could tell there were other patients and visitors in the room. My parents sat by my bedside. I tried to act a little bit cheerily, I was all cried out by now, though deep inside I was still burning up with questions. Dad had already made phone calls informing all who needed to know about what had befallen me. Of course he had also not come into terms with it. He would say it, not believing it was coming from his mouth. He then left soon afterwards to get us some dinner. I kept asking Mum how the room looked. She tried describing it as best she could so that I would at least have a vague idea of my new surroundings. She told me that the room was big and white with one wooden entrance door and two smaller doors leading to the balcony. There were six beds which were all occupied. There was one bathroom and toilet as well. I closed my eyes as she described the room for it was too painful to open them and not see a thing, just plain darkness. I could feel the gentle evening breeze from the ocean blow through the balcony doors and I knew that the ocean was close by. Mum confirmed my speculations. The other visiting relatives of my new roommates asked Mum what I was suffering from. Mum explained, trying not to stumble over her words with sobs. I could tell she was struggling to explain as she, just like me, did not want to believe it was actually true. They pitied me and I could tell they were staring at me, probably shaking their heads in disbelief. They told me that I was going to be okay even though I am sure they did not know if they believed it themselves. Dad came back with the food and he made me eat a lot. I wasn't feeling that hungry but trust me you can't convince my Dad of that. Dad, just like me, is a persistent person and does not take no for an answer. He is a businessman but I usually tell him he should have been a lawyer, perhaps that is why I have always had a passion for law. Mum didn't eat, this didn't surprise us. If my Mum doesn't eat it can only be three things; either she prepared the dish herself and lost appetite after cooking, or she is fasting, or she is stressed. In this case, the latter applied, who could blame her? Her daughter had gone blind and there were no answers to the numerous questions. Dad ate, I don't know how much but he ate in order to encourage me to eat. He later called the neurosurgeon to have a look at me. From their conversation, it seemed that the doctor would not be available till the next day. This was so frustrating. How was I going to sleep not knowing what I was suffering from? How fatal was it? Could it get worse? I complained to Mum although I knew she wouldn't have any answers for me. Uncle Andrew and Aunt Lucy dropped by later. From their silence I could tell they were shocked beyond belief. After all they had seen me the previous day and I had been okay! Or rather, seeing!

The time came for visitors to leave. Dad said a prayer, no, actually he cried to God asking Him to shed some light on my predicament. I shed some tears, too during the prayer for it was too painful hearing my father send this plea. Although he tried to be strong for me and Mum deep within he was hurting and broken. They left leaving Mum and me behind. I felt bad for Dad for he was going to spend the night alone in the lonely hotel room, enveloped in uncertainties. Mum tried to make me comfortable for the night ahead. I dozed off soon after of course not without getting a lullaby from the countless mosquitoes that seemed to have one agenda and that was to irritate people! I woke up several times in the night hoping that my sight would be back, boy was I wrong! I kept waking up and hearing the gentle snores of my newly acquired roommates. Mum was dead asleep, and I didn't want to wake her up. She had had a long day. One no mother would have ever wished for.

Finally, it was daybreak, I knew this from the birds chirping thousands songs of praise. Since my eyes had failed me, my ears were keener than before. The room soon came to life. There was only one shower. So it was a first-come, first-served basis. Mum wasn't comfortable with me stumbling and knocking things everywhere so she preferred we go to the hotel we had checked in to get ready there. That was a fantastic idea. We then had breakfast together with Dad before heading back to the hospital in time for the doctor's round checkup. He came asking me how I was that morning. I told him I was much better although I still could not see. He then prescribed some tablets in the meantime to help ease any pain. The neurosurgeon came in later. He asked me to narrate how I had been feeling before the blindness. I tried to explain everything and Mum would chip in once in a while if I forgot to mention something. He then examined my eyes and noted almost the same things as Dr Mataka had the previous day. Then he dropped a bombshell when he said,

"The way I see it, she must have brain surgery."

Have you been in a situation where you feel like screaming your lungs out but at the same time your body is too weak to even move a muscle? Well that is what I felt as soon the words left his mouth, having previously heard of a case of a surgery blunder where two patients who shared the same first name had had their operations mixed up. The one who was admitted for a knee operation had head surgery instead, while the other one who suffered from chronic migraine had unplanned knee surgery.

"Doctor, are you sure there is no other way to go about this?" I asked after regaining my poise.

"I'm afraid there isn't." He replied confidently.

Things started flashing before me. What if the surgery fails and I don't wake up from the operating table? What if I become paralyzed after the surgery? And yeah, how about my hair, I had put a lot into getting it where it was. Okay maybe that isn't such a strong point but it applies. The doctor requested me to take another CT scan and an MRI scan for further review. Saturday, 12 January was a public holiday, there was gaiety all round as people commemorated Zanzibar Revolution Day, but to me, my world had fallen apart. To say the least, the facilities were not available due to the holiday. Dad went to explain the seriousness of my situation but the answer was the same.

"We can't work today because it's a holiday. So you have to wait till Monday since Sunday is still a weekend."

Are you kidding me, does my illness know it's a holiday or weekend? The people for the MRI were even more depressing,

"I'm sorry sir but the soonest we can fit her in for an appointment is Tuesday."

"What? Not even for an emergency case?" Dad persistently pleaded with them. But they would not change their minds. That was absolutely unreasonable and to make it worse, there was only one MRI facility in the whole city! So it was either to take it or leave it.

I mean my life suddenly had a blackout and no one was caring enough to do anything to find out exactly what was wrong? Protocol is good but doesn't protocol have a place for real human feelings? Honestly, these radiologists, if their son, daughter, spouse, mother or father was in my situation would they still say, "I'm sorry but it has got to wait." I don't think so. I was seething with anger on the inside. I kept asking myself these questions without saying them out loud. It was only Saturday, I never thought Monday would ever come! Time usually flies by if there is some activity going on so I prayed for that. Relatives and friends came in that weekend. Everyone who got the call and was in Dar tried to avail themselves. For most, they had to kill their curiosity that it was actually me and that I actually couldn't see. I had to let my friends in Nairobi and everywhere else know, so that's where my cousin Chaya came in. I would dictate the message and he would diligently write and send it.

I then called him my PS (Personal Secretary) for he was responsible for handling my calls and messages. My friends were shocked, they couldn't believe it. So they actually called to confirm. I even spoke to Miss Tuimur, who had been my English teacher back in high school. She was shocked and couldn't believe it either. But as usual she was very encouraging with her catch phrase, "Never say die!" Due to the political crisis in Kenya, our neighbouring country to the north, at that time schools had delayed in their opening. So I even informed my school going friends; for I studied in Kenya both for my primary and secondary. They wanted to cry, they asked me over and over again if I knew what I was saying. I told them to pray for me because prayer is the only answer. I even let my school matron know, dear old Miss Karanja. She inquired, like everyone else what had really happened. She told me not to worry and to be strong and that she would let my former housemates know as soon as they returned to school. Due to my unexpected condition I never witnessed the political wrangle in Kenya, which claimed the lives and homes of many people. It was something I kept hearing about but never saw; maybe it was a good thing because from what I heard, it was a tragic sight that shook even the strongest of men. I also informed my church elder back in Nairobi, Elder Rodgers, being a very inspiring leader he told me that God was in full control. Knowing that there were so many people crying to the Lord because of me, I did not doubt His healing power upon me. My parents have brought us up to be God-fearing people. We share our faith in God with a large community of family, friends and even strangers. Hence as soon as most people heard of my predicament, they turned to God in prayer. I then confessed my sin of asking God why I was in that situation. My heart was more at ease. I even began laughing again.

My brother Evarist, at the time, was in Bradford University, England, in his final year. If there is someone who I am in no doubt was overwhelmed with fright when informed of my situation, it was him; because when I talked to him over the phone and told him I was doing okay, he would not understand. How was I okay when I could not see? When I passed him over to speak to Mum, she even made it so hard for him to believe. Her answer was similar to mine and added that I was the last thing he should be worrying about. This may have looked unfair to him but it was to let him concentrate on his studies. He didn't believe Mum for we all know her as the type who conceals the seriousness of a problem until it has reduced then she tells you how serious it had been afterwards. So when Mum tried to reassure him, it made him feel worse for he knew things were not as she wanted them to appear.

However, Steven, his long time friend, had come to visit me and told him otherwise. For as soon as he saw me, he somehow went into panic. I could hear him walk in the room, then standing a step away from me as if gawking with his mouth hanging open.

"Maggie, I'm so sorry!" he said in a low sympathetic voice.

"I'm sorry, but who is this?" I asked hesitantly.

"It's Steven!" he answered, as shocked to see me as I was to hear him. Steven had been involved in a near-death accident which caused his right arm to be amputated from the elbow. I had not seen him since the incident so we were catching up and feeling sorry for each other's predicament. As the conversation wore on, I heard him searching for something in his pocket, which I soon discovered was his phone, for he soon excused himself to make a call.

"Hallo? Evarist, is that you?"

That is when I knew who he was calling. I could not stop him from talking to Evarist for he had moved to the balcony and I could only hear him faintly. He continued.

"Yes, Evarist mate... this is Steven, calling from Dar. Hallo? Can you hear me! I wonder why you are still in England and your sister has gone totally blind. Hallo? Can you hear me now? You've got to come..."

I guess the call was disconnected, perhaps the network was congested or something for the conversation ended. He came back and I told him he shouldn't have told Evarist for I knew he was going to be a nervous wreck. He just told me it was only fair for Evarist to know the truth rather than hearing it elsewhere. Steven left shortly afterwards and promised to drop by some other time.

Evarist was taking the next flight back home despite what Mum and I had said to make everything seem okay. The thing with being an only girl in the family of three boys is that one is treasured so much. My condition was a big blow to all my brothers. Raphael and Lucky were still at home in Musoma but they too insisted on coming to Dar. I was their only sister so if I had gone blind, where would the cows come from? That's an African saying, meaning they would not receive a dowry for I might never get married. Marriage is something highly treasured and respected in African culture. A married woman has her place in society and is valued and respected. I may only have been 19, but I had plans of getting married eventually. Now with this new blow came limitations, who would want to have a blind wife? Or how would I know how my husband looks?

Then there is Kenneth Limen, a good friend of the family. He is Cameroonian but works in Dubai. As soon as he heard the news, he went on the internet to research about what it could be and what could be done. He even went to ask his doctor about what it might be. He never stopped calling to find out about my progress. When he asked my mum all she said was

"Maggie is okay. She is going to be fine."

Ken wasn't going to have any of that and he asked,

"How can she be okay if she cannot see, Mama?"

My mum was lost for words. He then caught her off guard when he said,

"Mama, I'm coming to Tanzania."

That was finality, he wasn't begging, he was telling! Mind you, he had been in Tanzania over Christmas and had even seen me and Lucky off to Taiwan. The weekend passed by as I had hoped. During the nights I would still open my eyes with the hope of my recovered sight, only to be mocked by the darkness.

Monday, 14th January, Mum helped me get ready to go for the CT scan as scheduled. Before we headed for the scan, I first had to go and see an eye professor at Muhimbili who had briefly examined me on the Saturday after the neurosurgeon had seen me. He told me to count the fingers he was supposedly holding up and then used a torch to look into my eye. I told him I could neither see the fingers nor the torch. He laughed as he said,

"You will be okay."

For some reason I imagined it was an evil laugh and the statement was just part of his job as a reassurance to worried patients like me. I imagined him to be one of those evil mad scientists in cartoons who would always perform experiments that backfired. I shuddered at this thought and told myself that he was the professor so he knew what he was saying. He then continued,

"I will prescribe you some injections every two days. They are vitamin A jabs which should help you see in no time."

"Thank you doctor," I said, "But how soon are we talking about?" After all, that was my greatest concern.

"Hopefully, soon, I can't put a time limit but just trust the medicine will work."

"That is not so encouraging," I thought, but I did not say it loudly lest I offend his years of experience and research! Nonetheless, there was a ray of hope that I would see again.

He then put me up for another appointment after a week. Later another doctor came to see me, a psychiatrist, prescribed by the neurosurgeon. I was really offended that the latter actually thought I had gone crazy and needed to be cross examined. I later found out that he even had the audacity to tell my parents that I was just pretending and that I was only attention seeking. Now who seeks attention by pretending to be blind? Surely this was a disgrace to his profession and all the years in medical school!

On the other hand, the psychiatrist seemed to be slightly more empathetic. She seemed to be a mature woman, probably in her late forties or early fifties. She asked me to talk about myself. If there is something I am not particularly good at, it is describing myself but then I had to. I told her I am the third born in a family of four children. I told her of my hobbies which include watching the sunrise and sunset, staring at a full moon, acting and directing plays, swimming, giving people advice and also meeting new people. Then she asked me about my school life. I told her all about my amazing friends and our experiences back in high school. She then inquired about my family. I spoke about them with so much pride, love and appreciation. Then she asked me to describe what Mum was wearing. I tried to feel it and then opened my eyes really wide in order to have an idea. I couldn't tell. She then asked Mum to move positions and asked me if I could tell where she had moved to in the room. I searched the room, it was pin-drop silent except for the gentle breeze blowing a curtain near the balcony window. After straining a bit, I pointed in a direction which I sensed she would be, after all blood is thicker than water. I was right. I don't know how long the session went on, but all I know is that I was not happy with it. The psychiatrist seemed content with my answers and concluded that I was normal (as if I had doubted that!) and that my problem was not in her field of specialty.

After she had left, Mum told me later how the neurosurgeon had come up with that crazy idea. She said that after seeing me the first time on Saturday, he called my parents and told them a couple of things. She also said that when the doctor spoke to me, he would stare hard at my unnoticing eyes, as though wondering what it was about them that had failed me. He seemed to doubt that I was blind at all and that it was just a ploy for sympathy and attention from apparent boyfriends. He said;

"This girl is just pretending, she is not blind. I have seen cases like hers before. She just wants attention. I'm sure she is having problems with boyfriends or something."

My mother could not contain her anger and displeasure so she retorted,

"So how do these apparent boyfriends cause her to become blind?"

"Well, maybe they dumped her. Try this today, don't stay here tonight. Just go to the hotel and leave her on her own, you will find she will do everything herself," he remarked.

"Doctor, with all due respect, I'm not going to leave my daughter all alone!" she remarked harshly.

At that point Mum told me how she was burning up with rage. Dad almost physically attacked the doctor for speaking such nonsense, for lack of a better word. He refrained from doing so since there weren't many neurosurgeons so the saying goes, 'You cannot bite the arm that feeds you.'

The doctor then continued, "The results from the scan show that there seems to be not much of a problem. The results are negative."

"So what do we do now as Maggie is still blind?" Dad asked, obviously not satisfied with the doctor's analysis.

"I suggest maybe now you see this preacher who performs miracles or even visit the 'traditional doctors' back in the bush." He replied seeming satisfied with his suggestion.

Mum decided to maintain her cool. For she told me had she not done that, she would have been worse than a wounded buffalo or a lioness that had lost her cub. In Swahili, there is a proverb, "Usiwadharau wakunga uzazi ungalipo". Directly translated it means "Do not despise the midwives for as long as there is still child bearing." My mum was not going to abuse the doctor because you never know maybe he would be the one to operate on me later on. It was disappointing though that a learned fellow like that could make such uneducated remarks.

The first ward I was admitted in did not have sufficient air circulation. The air conditioner had broken down. Picture a room with five occupied hospital beds, visitors, nurses and doctors and no air conditioning. The room was so stuffy, humid and uncomfortable. The more I stayed in that room, the more frustrated and restless I became. We had to ask if there was a better conditioned room. We were in luck; they had one on the third floor. There wasn't a minute to spare, we moved that very hour. The shifting was arranged by the hospital matron who seemed to be a kind and warm elderly woman. She would always drop by in the mornings to ask about my night and wish me a good night before she left work in the evenings. In my darkness I tried to visualize how she looked, may be a medium-height, plump, slightly wrinkled woman. This image was scraped off when she touched my hand in order to greet me, she was wrinkled alright but definitely not plump for I could feel her lean fingers. As a sign of respect I had to stand up when greeting her and that is when I noticed she was shorter than me.

In my new room I was the only patient for one night. That night mum read a verse from the Bible for me. I had missed reading already. We then sang some hymns; since I did not know all of them by heart Mum would tell me the next line in advance so we could sing together. Such little moments brought us closer together, for she had become my eyes. The next day more patients arrived, each with their own problems. I was just glad the room was very well air-conditioned.

Since this room was not very different from the other one, I would try making my way around, of course I would stumble on a few things here and there. Mum would want to escort me, but I would tell her that I wanted to do it on my own. She would be reluctant but would let me go anyway, of course not without keeping a keen eye on me for as soon as I stumbled on something she would rush to my side and guide me the rest of the way. In the evenings I received a full body massage from a family friend to help ease the tension I felt in my neck, on the temples, right hand and back. It would put me to sleep almost immediately. Before the massage I would be taken for a walk by Chaya and Aunt Lucy, round the hospital and also to the public grounds adjacent to the hospital. The walks were always very relaxing and refreshing after being in bed almost the whole day. My aides would describe the surroundings, the leafy tree branches, the different birds that swooped around us, the noisy cars that zoomed past as we strolled along. There were also people who would stare in my direction shaking their heads and most of all the golden sunset that I missed so much. I would smile as they described how the fading embers of the setting sun seeped through the branches. While the gentle evening breeze ruffled the leaves, and the birds slowly flew off to their nests in preparation for the night. I sighed as we headed back to the hospital, glad that I had taken the walk, but sad that I could not see it for myself.

Some nights I would not sleep at all. I would toss and turn, just like the way I had been before I had gone blind. I remember one night I cried out in pain, squeezing Mum's hand in the hope of easing the pain. She gently patted my back in order to soothe me. I could hear some of the other people in the room whispering among themselves as I had woken them up with my cries. One of them was kind enough to go and call the nurse for I could not let go of Mum's hand. My neck was again driving me crazy despite the massage I had received earlier. I sat up, lay down, knelt on the bed and even stood up, but no position seemed comfortable enough. It was so bad that I requested an injection in the neck! The nurses laughed but I was very serious the tablets seemed to be a waste of time. I thought that an injection in the neck would be a quicker and surer remedy. They gave me one, though it was on my bum. It still worked and fast, I soon relaxed and tried to get some sleep as Mum gently rubbed my back so as to soothe me and lull me to sleep.

Just when so me decent sleep had come, the pain started all over again. It was as if the injection had never taken place. The same drill was on, tossing, turning, kicking, crying and shifting back and forth. I cried for another injection but they wouldn't give me one because I had just had one. They gave me painkillers instead. I almost threw them away. I cried to God to alleviate the pain so that I could get some sleep. He did, in no time I was dead asleep.

Every night at around 3am Dad would call from the hotel and pray with us. He would pray for almost an hour. I would stifle a cry, as he implored the heavenly Father to bestow healing upon me. I would fall asleep more at ease after he hung up. Every single night without fail, he would call and pray with us. Mum would kneel by my bedside as I sat up with my hands clasped together. I knew Dad was also kneeling back in the hotel room, probably with his Bible in one hand and the phone in the other. Prayer was the only thing that kept us going, for the doctors did not shed any light on the situation.

Thursday, January 17, we were just talking with Mum, Dad, Chaya, and Agnes when Kenneth walked in and surprised us. I only realized he was there after Mum screamed, "Ken!" I was confused and tried to search in the darkness to see if I could spot him. I couldn't. He had come, all the way from Dubai to Dar, not just Dar, to the hospital and into the ward. He came to my bedside and hugged me. He was quiet for a moment, I guess he was still processing the reality of my situation. Mum later told me his silence was due to the fact that he had stretched out his hand in greeting but I had not seen it. I had just stared into the direction Mum had screamed from, oblivious of Ken's outstretched arm. I told him I was doing fine and asked about how he had found the place for no one had known he was coming. Laughter filled the room soon after. We were all happy to see him, well not literally see him, but I was glad he was around. He had brought with him a small pharmacy if I may call it that. He had a selection of vitamin tablets, nutritional foods and anything healthy he could lay his hands on. I could tell my bedside table was overflowing as Mum arranged the things and requested a stool to put the extra things on. He also brought an enlarged baby photo of mine when I was a month old. I struggled to see it but I couldn't because I was told not to strain my eyes. I really wanted to see it even though I knew what the original photo looked like. I made sure it stayed by my bedside so that the day I opened-no-the day my eyes would be opened I would see it. In the meantime I would only feel the texture of the frame and hug it tightly.

The day before had not been a good one; I had felt really weak. The lab results showed I was anemic, just like in Taiwan. I was told to eat a lot of nutritive diets and was also given certain syrups to help increase the blood. Eating was a big problem because I never had any appetite most of the time. Or if I ate most of the time I would just throw up. I would even cry sometimes because I did not want food. Dad even took the initiative of feeding me himself. It was like I was a child again. He would encourage me by saying that there was a small portion left so I should just eat. And I did only to discover the portions were never ending. Other times I would ask if I could feed myself, and they let me, but I ended up spilling the food on my clothes or even missing the food on the plate so there was always someone to direct the spoon in the right direction. In order to entice me to eat more, Ken came with honey and cinnamon, of which he said I should take a cup daily. It was to help with relaxing the nerves.

Friday January 18, I had an appointment with the eye professor. The appointment was scheduled for 10am but we ended up seeing him at around 1pm. As we waited Ken vented his anger about how messed up our health system was. I agreed with him. We complained of the way a week down the line no doctor had told me exactly what I was suffering from. We vented our anger about how that particular doctor was so late and no one was telling us his whereabouts. We complained of the heat and just about everything. Mum sat by me just listening to us go on and on with our patience running low as time went by. Dad kept frantically going to ask the nurses when the doctor would show up. Each time they would say he was on his way. Ken then suggested that maybe we should start thinking of getting help from abroad. He said,

"Here the doctors will dilly dally and tell you nothing, but when things get out of hand they will tell you, 'Sorry Mama for your loss.'"

"Ken, we will think about your proposal." Mum replied calmly.

The more we talked the more my anger boiled within me. It felt as though the doctors were gambling with my life since none of them had said anything helpful. As the conversation wore on, I then heard some familiar voices and it was not Mum, Dad or Ken. It was my brothers, Raphael and Lucky! They gave us a surprise by showing up at the hospital and I was so happy to have them around. Lucky could not believe that I couldn't see so he made fun of me. He said things like, "Maggie, why are you not looking straight at me, your eyes are facing different directions!" or "How many fingers am I holding up?" I guess he would play around with his fingers when he said this. At one point he was showing me something on his phone and would insist I looked at it. Mum then told him to stop tormenting me. I did not feel offended, I understood him, after all we had been together in Taiwan! As for Raphael, I could tell he was shocked beyond reason. He just embraced me tightly for a long time and did not say a word. Knowing him well, I knew he was hurting deep within. He doesn't say much when he is deep in thought. He probably had folded his arms across his chest with one hand stretching up to his neck looking completely helpless. I tried to reassure him that I would be fine, but he knew I was trying to cheer him up.

Shortly afterwards I was called in by the doctor. My frustration had cooled down by this time for I was so glad my brothers were there. As Mum and Dad led me into the room, I could feel the cool chill from the air conditioner and the strong scent of the eye professor hit me. I had become so accustomed to the darkness that I began noticing some motion in front of me after I got used to new surroundings. It was as though when there is a sudden blackout, at first it is pitch black, but with time one is able to grope around in the darkness and somehow get used to it. There were other people in the room apart from the professor. I could not tell how many they were or where they were standing. I soon found out that it was a group of his students. He started by examining me then asked them to follow suit. I felt like some kind of specimen in the laboratory under examination. After that he asked each of them to explain what they had seen in my eyes and what they thought my problem was. Each student trying to please their master replied as best as they could remember from their classes! At the back of my head I could not help wonder what these students thought as they saw me there. The professor then asked me if I had noticed any improvement from the last time he had attended to me. I told him that I was getting used to the darkness. He laughed while patting my back and said,

"I told you, you will be fine. Just keep taking the injections and in no time you will be well."

I faked a smile. Deep within me I felt like I should tell him off, first for letting me wait for that long and then for him making the situation a comedy! I spared him being humiliated in front of his students and left the room with my parents who were just as little amused.

We went back to Hope Hospital in silence. When we got there, one of my aunts, Mama Nyalali, suggested that we should visit an eye hospital, Comprehensive Community Based Rehabilitation Centre (CCBRT). That idea was put on hold. Since the major hospital had failed, what would this centre do?

My Dad's cousin, Uncle Peter and his wife, Betty also came to visit at the ward. My uncle had been preparing to go back to America when the news reached him. He decided that, he had to see me before leaving or else his conscience would not let him travel in peace. They were speechless when they walked into the room and stretched out their hands to greet me, but I only stared blankly until Mum took my hand and guided it to their outstretched ones. They were speechless, because we had been together during

Christmas back at the village, where I was full of life and glad to see family members whom I hadn't seen in a while. It had been a great family reunion, sadly I might never see all of them again. That thought made my stomach churn. Uncle Peter has a significant bald spot which I always made fun of. He told me that when I regained my eyesight it would have grown hair again. I just laughed for he always made such jokes. Before he flew off, he suggested we should inform him if we were thinking of going for treatment abroad. He left a day later but his wife stayed on for an extra two days before heading back to Arusha. After Aunt Betty left Mum told me how the former had tears in her eyes every time she looked at me groping around in my darkness. That is Aunt Betty for you, she is quite an emotional person. My other uncle, Josephat, Peter's brother, had also come to visit us together with his wife. They were all so saddened on seeing me there, helpless.

Mama Nyalali would come with food and also read some encouraging Bible scriptures. She would tell me to claim God's promises at that very crucial moment. Although I had not seen her in four years, she seemed no different. Her laughter resounded around the room and she always held my hand when talking to me. Sometimes she came with Lulu, her niece, also a very charming and enthusiastic person. They would always make me eat so much. One cannot say no to my aunt for she has this imploring tone and a warm encouraging smile that would just make you do as she says. I could not see the smile but I could imagine it, so I ate. I received so many visitors it cheered me up. Family members, friends, family friends, all dropped in to show their support. That is what I love the most about African culture. One is never alone. We bear each other's burdens, when one of us is hurting, we all hurt. We are each other's shoulder to lean on. Thus my darkness had become their darkness as well. They never at once wanted me to feel I was all alone or that my parents were alone. I was a child of the community thus the community carried me as a whole. That is why most of my characters are referred to as either aunt or uncle, this is a polite way of addressing my elders, and not all of them are blood relatives. Aunt Norah (a friend of my Aunt Anna, Dad's cousin, who lives in the USA) also came with her husband and niece, Scola. They would bring a lot of nutritious meals and Scola would keep me company and guide me as I ate. Even though we had never met before, I felt a strong liking towards her. There was also my long lost Uncle Jimmy who hadn't seen me since I was one year old. I could not remember how he looked and this was not the appropriate time to figure that out. I was just glad he had come. He came with my cousin Maganga, whom I hadn't seen also in a long time. I always had so many visitors that the nurses had to chase them away sometimes, for they were crowding up the room.

My aunts, Mum's friends, Angelina, Mama Maurine and Mama Aggie were really good at bringing food for they believed if someone was sick, food was to be the first cure. They would bring food at different times on different days. However, at times they would clash and all bring food at once so my stomach had no choice but to accept all and sundry. I was constantly fed all because I had lost weight and was anemic. My cousins, Rose, John and Tina from Dad's eldest brother came too. We hadn't seen each other in a while also. They were great company, we talked and laughed and just forgot I was sick and everything was back to normal. However that did not change the fact that I couldn't see them.

Many of Dad's friends also came. I cannot remember all of them but I remember Uncle Mashauri and his wife who would show up whenever they could. Then there was Dr. Bwana, a long-time family friend who turned up almost as soon as he heard the news. Let the title not fool you, he is no medical doctor, just a doctor of the law. He is always soft spoken but authoritative. Wisdom always seemed to leave his mouth whenever he speaks. The white hairs on his head are proof of the wisdom he possesses. His silence was an indication that he did not know what to say that would make the situation seem okay. He held my hand between his broad, aging but firm hands and just kept silent. I don't know if he was staring at me or he was saying a silent prayer, there was just silence for a while before he let go of my hand. I could picture him immaculately dressed in an African print shirt, "Kitenge" for he loved wearing them. He came along with his lovely daughter, Tina whom I had last seen in 2004. Dr. Bwana is my role model, for I have always been passionate about studying Law, so he always encouraged me. He always used to say:

"Your big law books are waiting for you!"

But this time he did not say that. It was as though he was deep in thought before I interrupted him and said,

"It seems like this is the end of the road for my law career." I smiled weakly as I said this, for it hurt deep inside that I would never be the first female Chief Justice of Tanzania or one of the Panel judges in the International Court of Justice (ICJ) in The Hague.

He was silent for a while before he muttered,

"Did you know that one of the greatest judges who ever lived was blind? So my dear, all hope is not lost. You can still achieve your dream."

My spirit was elevated by this, at least I would achieve my childhood dream. However the thought of learning Braille dampened my spirits again. "How will I even start?" I asked myself. I brushed that thought quickly aside for I was hoping to see again.

Tina and I would talk about everything; school, news, fashion, music, movies, food, boys, Musoma, our hometown and just about everything. It was amazing how we had so much in common, like our birthdays which were two weeks apart, similar music, strong faith in God. She would ask if I needed anything that would make my hospital stay more comfortable like a radio or extra pillows. I thanked her and told her I was alright. I really enjoyed her company and would feel a bit sad whenever she had to leave. I would look forward to her visits for she had new stories from the world of the seeing. There was also Mzee Masua, Dr. Bwana's father. Unfortunately he passed on even before this book was published. He would come, greet me then sit by my bedside and not say a word. He, just like his son, was a man of few words. He wasn't alien to dealing with a blind person for his wife had unfortunately lost her sight a few years previously. Before he left, he would tell me everything was going to be ok. I wished I could see him and just be amazed at how father and son resembled each other. It always made me happy looking at Dr. Bwana and his father, both advanced in age with grey hair and similar smiles. All these people made my stay at the hospital less lonely and less frightening. I had become more familiar with the darkness. I was less clumsy when I walked, either because I was used to the place or because Mum had cleared my path for me so I did not have any obstacles on the way. Either way, I stumbled on fewer items.

Sunday, 20 January, I was eagerly waiting for my eldest brother Evarist to fly in from England. He was not going to be left out on this out of the ordinary event so he asked for an immediate leave off work and school so as to be with the rest of the family. He came in while I was resting, so Mum had to wake me up and ask me to guess who it was. I sat on the bed, unsuccessfully trying to peek through the sheer darkness while listening as he slowly drifted towards me, his movement flowed with such surreal grace. I screamed, "Evarist!"

"Maggie, my dear, you're blind!" he cried in a jocular manner. His voice was a bit quaky as he heaved a soft sigh. We embraced each other for a long time until Lucky complained that I had not hugged him for that long.

We went outside to the balcony and talked and laughed. He asked how I was holding up and I told him I was great. Of course he didn't believe that, but he did not dissent either. Then Ken decided to capture the moment as we laughed and joked about things, with his camera. He also took a family photo, which took a lot of trial and error since I could not look straight at the camera. He kept taking a couple of shots until he was satisfied that I was looking at the camera. With Evarist around, the family was complete. None of us had anticipated a family reunion that soon. Although we had been brought together by a painful situation, it was still a blessing in disguise being with my whole family, whom I hold so dear. From there onwards, for all the appointments which followed, I would drag all my brothers along, including Chaya and Ken. It felt like a royal escort.

That evening we all had dinner together at a nearby restaurant. It was great. The place was filled with laughter that drowned the soft background classical music. People were catching up on the latest issues and remembering good old times. There was a slight, chilly evening breeze, but it was no match for the warmth that emerged from the company of loved ones. I even heard my parents laugh, I had not heard them laugh since the incident. It was a good night to forget the bad things and dwell on the good ones.

During the following week things took a different twist. Raphael and Lucky left for Musoma on Monday morning. I missed them as soon as they had left. I then remembered how on one of my evening walks with the two of them, Lucky had been so busy texting and Raphael had momentarily looked away. I presumed that they did not see me hit a lamp post. I was slightly annoyed since they had not warned me. Another time, Lucky was telling me to look at some birds that were up on a tree. I looked at him and asked rhetorically, "What part of 'I cannot see' don't you understand?" I missed them for such little things.

Monday 21st January, we finally went to CCBRT- Dad, Mum, Evarist, Ken and I. It was annoyingly hot so everyone's mood was slightly irritable. As soon as we got there I got registered and was soon attended to by an optician. After some tests, finger counting and object identification - which turned out to be disappointing, he referred me to his superior who requested for some blood tests to be done. After the results came back he questioned me about my condition. He then honestly told me that my problem was beyond him and he called on his superiors as well to have a look at me. We were led into a different room which seemed a bit small for we walked through a narrow corridor and through a narrow door and only Mum and I were allowed in, the rest had to wait outside. It also felt a bit crowded and slightly poorly ventilated for I sometimes felt like I lacked air. There were other patients in the room for I could hear babies crying and mothers shushing them. Apart from that, I could not tell if there was anything else. Of course I imagined there were chairs and maybe tables cluttered with paperwork and some equipment for conducting tests. When the doctors had a look at me they said things like,

"It looks like there is a hemorrhage in the eye; the optic discs are serrated; the optic nerve seems pale," and many other medical terms. I did not cry this time like I had done the first day when the blackout struck. I just listened as they went on about how horrible the inside of my eyes looked.

After the examination they told me to come back the next day so that their boss, who was out for surgery that day, could have a look at me. We left looking forward to the next day, for maybe there would be some answers, I just prayed within me for answers. It was frustrating enough not knowing.

We headed back to the hospital to find Aggie and her mum there. We had lunch together as more visitors dropped in later in the day. Despite the people who were around, the place seemed a bit quiet. Perhaps because Raphael and Lucky had left there was no one to disturb me or maybe I was getting sick and tired of the same routine every day. The day dragged on until the last group of visitors left and Mum and I retired off to bed.

Tuesday, 22nd January, early in the morning we left for CCBRT again. We had to get there on time so that we would see the doctor as early as possible. After being checked in, we were put in the register to see the chief doctor. As we waited, I continued praying that not only would he/she tell me what was wrong, but also how I would be treated and more importantly, whether I would see again. I was called in, that was the moment of truth, I thought. His voice sounded familiar, it was like someone I had heard not so long before. Then it hit me, it was one of the doctors who had examined me the first day at Muhimbili.

Mum confirmed my suspicions for she had seen him that day. She later told me how at that initial stage her heart sank, for this doctor hadn't said anything the last time so what would be different this time. As soon as Mum helped me to my seat, he remarked,

"Wait a minute, I remember you. Weren't you at Muhimbili about a week ago?"

"Yes, I was," I answered enthusiastically.

"That's right, I remember your case," he continued, "Actually I have been researching into it. Just give me a minute, I'll get my book." He concluded and left the room almost hastily.

I felt somewhat relieved. That was something we hadn't heard before, someone had actually spent his time researching into my case! He came back shortly; I could hear him flip through some pages and then he said:

"Margareth, your condition is caused by excess cerebral fluid in the brain, which causes the swelling of the optic nerve, which may lead to loss of vision, as in your case."

Bang! There it was at last. He did not beat around the bush. He just put us in the know almost immediately. I had been blind for 11 days and no one had said anything to shed some light on my condition all that time, and this doctor summarized it in less than a minute! I was happy, not because I had just found out that my brain fluid had increased, but because I knew that once the problem had been identified, the solution would soon follow. I thanked God. Mum, too, praised God. The doctor went on to say:

"For starters, we need to test for the pressure in the spinal fluid through a process called acupuncture."

As he said this, I heard him ruffle a paper and click a pen and begin writing down a prescription that I was to use before the procedure was done. He spoke with a matter of urgency as he wrote it down. I stopped him before he could finish writing and asked him to explain how the exact procedure was going to be carried out, for it was a bit too much to take in at once. He said,

"It is a simple procedure. They take a sample of the spinal fluid by inserting a syringe at the end of the spine and draw it out."

I shuddered at the thought of a syringe going through my spine so I asked,

"Is it a delicate procedure?"

"Yes it is. It requires utmost concentration for if the neurologist messes up a bit, it could lead to serious neural complications and in the worst case scenario-paralysis."

I needed a moment to take it all in and to consult with Mum, Dad and the rest who were waiting outside. After much deliberation, Mum asked the doctor if he would recommend us to go abroad for treatment since we were a bit skeptical about having such a delicate procedure done there. He suggested the U.K; I could tell from his accent that he was British so he could not help suggest his home country. He also suggested South Africa, for it has good medical facilities and it is cheaper than the U.K.

"What about the USA?" I asked and noticed he had stopped writing.

"It is really good as well; they are more advanced than the UK and South Africa. In fact I would recommend it if you know someone there."

"I have relatives over there, so I guess it would be better than the other two countries," I replied confidently.

He offered to write a letter to the embassy to help with our visa process. He told us to go and collect the letter next day. We were so grateful, we kept showering him with gratitude and prayers of prosperity and long life. God had opened a window when all other doors were closed. We had underestimated this doctor but he turned out to be the greatest help. As we walked out he called after me and said,

"Make sure you get all other documents ready, for you need to get medical attention as soon as possible."

I nodded and thanked him again. I really wished I could see him, I pictured him to be a Caucasian, tall, medium-size, maybe late thirties or early forties in age, slightly wrinkled, with a tan, depending on how long he had been under the African sun. It didn't matter that I could not see him. At least he helped me and he knew I was grateful.

We shared the good news with the rest. They were glad as well. Evarist was told to book the visa appointment that evening. Dad contacted my uncle and aunt in the America for the necessary documents. After leaving the hospital Ken invited us for lunch at his hotel as he was leaving for Dubai that afternoon. He was glad that there was some progress so he felt confident that things would be okay when he left. The lunch was exquisite. The subtle classical music in the background and warm gentle breeze from the ocean nearby complimented the array of cuisine from the buffet. Evarist selected food for me as I sat at the table trying to take in the new surroundings. I decided to share my thoughts with Evarist. I commented,

"The orange colour of the room compliments well with the serene atmosphere."

"What orange colour?" Evarist asked, slightly bemused.

"The one painted on the walls of course." I replied confidently pointing to the wall nearest to me.

He laughed, "It's not orange. It's a combination of cream and off-white," he corrected.

"Oh! It looks like orange in my world." I laughed at myself.

"Maybe you should suggest it to them to repaint the place" he said jokingly. The rest just laughed.

It was not the first time I had had a colour blindness encounter. I had started noticing some colours a few days back. I could only notice some colours from the corner of my eye. This was exciting since my world was not pitch black anymore. It was as though I had put on some very dark sunglasses which blocked the bright light and only some colours seeped in. Unfortunately, for most of the time, I was wrong about the colours that I could see. One time we had gone to visit Dr. Bwana's place and I remembered the last time I was there the house had been white. This time however, before me stood a pink house! I nudged Evarist and asked,

"Wasn't this house white the last time? Why did they paint it pink?"

"Maggie, it is still white!" he corrected, amused of course.

"Hmm, believe it or not it appears pink to me. My colour co-ordination is interesting, I tell you," I said laughing at myself.

Another time Mum and I were in the ladies room and I commented that the olive green colour of the walls was so not appropriate. Mum politely told me,

"No dear, the bathroom is actually royal blue and white!"

My family made a joke out of this. Whenever we would go somewhere they would ask,

"Maggie, what is the colour of the day?"

I would just laugh and tell them what I could honestly see that day and they would burst out laughing if I was way off. It was funny how we had turned this grim situation into laughter.

After lunch, Dad thanked Ken, on behalf of the family, for taking his time off work to come and be with us during that tough period. Ken being as humble as always just remarked,

"Papa, it was my pleasure. We are all family and family sticks together through the good and the bad times."

Ken then checked out and we got into different taxis, his to the airport and ours back to Hope Hospital. On arrival, we requested for a discharge and we were granted one. There was no use continuing with the admission since there had been no significant help received there. I would miss the matron and the nurses though, who had grown fond of me.

When I say God exists I know what I am really talking about. When dad went to pay the bill he was told it was already paid.

"Who paid?" He inquired, absolutely puzzled.

"I'm sorry sir, but we were asked not to reveal the identity of the person. Let's just say it is a Good Samaritan," the nurse replied with a discreet smile, probably glad she had contained the secret.

My dad came back and told us the news. We were all equally puzzled and asked each other who it could be since there were just so many people who had come to visit me at the hospital. We individually thanked God for that miracle and prayed for whoever the angel was. I never got to know who the Good Samaritan was, but God knows he or she has a special place in our hearts. I took one dark, blurred glance around the room that had housed me for the last couple of days and sighed. As we passed the reception desk, I went over, since I frequently passed it when going for my evening walks, and bid the nurses farewell. I could just recognize them by their voices, so they made the effort of reaching for my hand to shake it. They all wished me a speedy recovery. Whether they believed it was possible or not I didn't know. At least they showed some concern.

With only Dad, Mum, Evarist, Chaya and I, it was somehow quiet. That evening Evarist and Chaya filled in the visa application forms, while the rest remained in the hotel everyone doing their own thing. Dad whistling a hymn, Mum sorting out our clothes for we had an unexpected trip coming up and me, well just sleeping since I could not watch the TV in my room. I had tried to watch it but all I could see was a flicker of lights and an array of mixed colours running horizontally across the screen. I moved so close until I was almost kissing the television set, but it did not help me. I just placed my hands over my eyes for I suddenly felt the pressure I had put on my eyes, they hurt slightly so Mum told me not to strain them. I just listened to the programs before taking a nap. I felt emotional since this was the first time since the incident that I had had to watch a TV. The reality of the situation was clear once more, I had become so used to it that I had not realized how it affected me in other aspects of my life. I shed a tear at the thought of never recovering my eyesight and how I would miss out on seeing so many things. I slept it off and encouraged myself to believe that I would get my eyesight back.

Wednesday, 23rd January, while having our breakfast, Dad, Mum, Evarist and I were approached by the waiters and waitresses inquiring how I was holding up. After telling them that I was going for further treatment, they said that their prayers were with us. Unlike the last time I was in that hotel, this time I ate my breakfast well, of course Mum kept a keen eye on me so that I didn't spill anything on my clothes.

After breakfast we went to CCBRT to pick up the letter addressed to the embassy. Evarist got in touch with Dr. Bowman, the ophthalmologist who had shed some light on my condition. He told him that we should go to his office as his secretary had all the details. He was held up attending to other patients. We were still thankful because he had put a lot of thought into my case and at least he was out there giving hope to another person who had none left.

We headed to his office. Miriam, his secretary, a middle-aged woman as Mum described to me later on, welcomed us. We explained the purpose for our visit. She said she had not been told anything so she had to call Dr. Bowman to inquire. From her responses, I could tell she was being instructed what to do, for I could hear her ruffle some paper as she jotted down something. As soon as she hung up, I heard the rattle of keys on the keyboard so I knew she was typing out something.

As she typed, I tried to study the room we were in. It smelt of fresh wood varnish, so it was a new office I could tell. The floor was cemented and without a carpet from the sound of our shoes clacking on it. It had a good air conditioner, so the room was not stuffy. There was a large mahogany table at the centre of the room for we were made to sit there as we waited. The other things in the room were all blurry, I even tripped on a sofa on the entrance to the office. Miriam then asked Mum what was wrong with me. Mum had to do the painful narration which she had still not gotten used to. Every time someone asked her, it was just as painful as the first time she had realized the reality of my condition. She played with my hand as she explained to Miriam, who I could tell had stopped typing for a while as she gasped, 'Jesus Christ!' and I guess she was shaking her head as she said this. After Mum finished narrating, Miriam was quiet for a while before asking us if she could pray for me before we left. We agreed, for at that point we accepted all the prayers as long as they were directed to our heavenly Father. Once she had finished typing she told us to return later that afternoon as the doctor would have signed and stamped it then. Then she began to pray, and pray she did. We then thanked her and headed back to the hotel.

Dad went about in town to run some errands in preparation for our soon to be trip. We had a lunch invitation that day so we had to get to the hotel before our hosts arrived. Dr. Bwana came to pick us up and we told him that Dad would join us later for he had been held up in town. We drove in silence to his place.

The lunch was delicious. We sat around the table, Dr. Bwana and his lovely wife, Angelika, Mum, Evarist, Tina, Anna; Tina's older sister with her son, Aaron, Robert-Tina's brother, and I. Mum thanked them for inviting us for lunch. Mrs. Bwana expressed how glad she was that we had come. She also told me that I was going to be fine after Mum told them what Dr. Bowman had said. The rest of the lunch was filled with laughter and positive criticisms of our lack of equipment and expertise in the health system. Later the adults went to the lounge leaving Evarist, Tina, Anna, Robert and I at the table talking about nothing in particular. Anna asked,

"So how much can you see now?"

"Well," I said as I felt for my glass of water. "Not much, although I can recognize the shape of someone or something."

"Can you tell the things on the table?" Tina asked.

"I can tell this is a glass because I am holding it," I said smiling, and they all laughed. I tried to look at the items they were mentioning, but all I could see was a pile of things. I could not pick any item out.

"Nope, it just looks like a dark pile to me. I can guess, but that is because I know we are at the table so I will just say, plates, cutlery, jug, serving bowls and glasses."

"Oh," Anna sighed.

"Oh, Maggie!" Tina echoed

"I'll be fine," I said smiling weakly.

The rest of the conversation turned to a celebrity who had committed suicide a few days back. Dad later came and joined the adults in the lounge. After a wonderful afternoon, we headed back to the hotel.

Evarist had managed to get us an appointment for the following day at the American embassy. Since the appointment was early in the morning, we had an early night. Somewhere in the night some unexpected, unexplainable thing happened. It felt like a strong battle between unforeseen forces in my room. My whole body felt like it was on fire. I thought maybe it was too hot in the room, so I just switched on the air conditioner. However, this was helpful only for a while and then I felt like it was too cold so I had to switch it off. When I did, the burning sensation returned. This battle went on for a while; I was sweating profusely, and panting from the nightmares I had had that seemed so real. I was afraid to open my eyes. I cried and prayed in bed as I tossed and turned and threw away my bedding for it felt like it was also on fire.

That feeling lasted for a while until I could not take it anymore and decided to dial my parents' room number. I opened my eyes slowly, the room was dark, with an eerie silence. I could hear cars drive past from a distance, there were also some voices of people going on with their business at night. I could not tell the time even though my phone was by my bedside. I tried to dial my parents' room number with the hotel phone. I knew their room extension number but I struggled finding the right numbers. I tried to remember how digits were positioned on telephones. After a couple of trials I finally managed to get hold of them. I was crying as I whispered that I needed her and Dad to come to my room for something creepy was happening. She told me to calm down and she would be there soon. Mum knocked and I stumbled in the dark to reach for the door to let her in. I told her about my experience. She went to get Dad. He came in and I narrated to him and he began praying, rebuking all powers of evil. He read a couple of scriptures from the Bible and we prayed again. They placed their hands on my head as we prayed. I felt more at peace after the prayers, and I slept soundly after they had left. I still can't explain why I felt that way that night. I was just glad it was over.

In the morning Mum helped me to get ready for the embassy. I had already been accustomed to being bathed even though I was 19. It felt like I was a child all over again. We did not even have time for breakfast since we had to get there in time. Evarist waited for us outside the embassy as Dad, Mum and I went in. The security check guards asked what was wrong with me. Mum summarily explained to them and they all pitied me and prayed that my application would be successful and eventually my treatment as well.   After so many security checks we were finally allowed in and we waited in the lounge for our names to be called. As we sat there, I prayed for them to grant us the visa. There was a TV somewhere in the room, for I could hear the news anchor read out the news. Mum was my eyes so she was telling me how people were nervous, each praying to their God. I could picture them, shifting the weight of one leg to the other, as they looked around the well-conditioned room. She also told me how they would sigh with relief, jump in excitement or dance a bit when their applications came through. One particular man, an evangelist, made us laugh when he told the consular official he was welcome to his church for he had been granted his visa. When we were called, Mum guided me to the counter and after answering a few questions and having our fingerprints taken, we were asked to wait as he further questioned Dad.

Then he concluded, "You can collect your visas tomorrow afternoon."

"Can we get them earlier than that since we have a flight booked for tomorrow morning?" Dad asked him, hoping to get a positive response.

"I'm sorry sir, but the soonest we can give them to you is in 24 hours. We could write you a letter to take to the ticket office so that they can change your flight."

"Thank you, that will be greatly appreciated," Dad responded.

"You can come back this afternoon and pick up the letter. Good luck with your trip and get well soon, Maggie," he concluded.

"Thank you," I said shyly.

We left the embassy excited, thanking God for granting us the visas. Now we knew the trip was before us. There was so much to do with so little time. First, Dad had to go to the ticket office to sort the tickets out, Mum and Evarist had to shop for warm jackets since we were going during the winter period in the USA. I had to braid my hair so before they left Mum dropped me off at a nearby salon and instructed them to be gentle with my head.

I could tell it was a small salon because it was stuffy and as I sat down to be braided, my feet were pushed against the door. The hairdressers kept asking me to move whenever they tried to get a thing or two in the room. I tried to familiarize myself with the room. I could see what seemed to be an orange curtain blowing from the slight breeze of cars that passed outside on the dusty road outside. There was a radio somewhere in the room blasting some Taarab songs; typical for most coastal people to listen to. There was a fan, but it wasn't working well enough so I felt like I was out of breath. As I sat there hoping time would go by, other customers came and left. There was the usual salon gossip and talk going on, I did not contribute since none of it concerned me. At that moment I really missed my phone, for normally I would be texting in a salon. I had my phone but I couldn't text. Then Aggie's mum came to keep me company since Mum had told her I would be there. I was glad at least I had someone to talk to. The hairdresser asked her what had happened to me. My aunt briefly told her.

This stirred up a hot debate. They began telling stories of witchcraft, and how their relatives and friends of friends had had something similar to my condition. They told me that even though I trusted God I should know that witchcraft existed and that I should pay a visit to some witchdoctors. Even one of the customers said that maybe a former schoolmate was getting back at me for doing well in school. I just smiled and said nothing. Their level of thinking was a bit too superstitious and I had been brought up not believing in such things. I would never go to a witchdoctor. The condition was medical and I trust God, for Him only do I serve.

I could not wait for my hair to be done with. Evarist and Chaya came in later to see my progress, they then waited outside when they were told I would not take long. We then paid and as I left they wished me a quick recovery. I was thankful. We went back to the hotel because Mum was packing. I wasn't of much help so I went to sit in the lobby with Evarist. The rest of the day just wore on. Dad managed to change the tickets to the red eye flight. He was not going to come with me and Mum, but he was going to join us later. Since my incident had been unexpected, he had had no time to organize things back at the office and also Lucky needed to join his first year of secondary school. Raphael needed tuition fees, for he was also soon going back to Australia. I really pitied Dad, for everyone was demanding something from him. I just prayed for God to give him the means to provide for all of us.

Friday, 25 January, Dad left early in the morning for the embassy to collect our passports. Friends and family came to bid us farewell at the hotel. Some came to bring some presents for their relatives in the States. I was with Tina the entire afternoon till the time we left for the airport. We sat in the lobby passing time. She told me to keep in touch and that she would be praying for me.

She even tested my sight one last time, by asking me to count the number of fingers she held up. I got almost all of them wrong even though I opened my eyes as wide as I could. All I could see was her hand waving from side to side but not the fingers. Tina then commented,

"Maggie you are not even looking at me!"

"What do you mean? I am staring right at you, or so I think," I replied, trying to focus my eyes in the direction her voice came from.

"Nope, both eyes are facing in different directions. It's like you are facing sideways."

"And now?" I asked as I tried to position my head differently and shifting my eyes.

"Mh-mh! Still sideways. Hey don't strain your eyes, my darling, you will get a headache."

"No wonder Lucky said my eyes are like a chameleon's!" I said, laughing.

It must have been uncomfortable for people to look directly at me. She encouraged me to be strong and told me I would be okay. Steven, Evarist's friend, were there too. He spent most of the time with Evarist and Chaya, but would occasionally join our conversation. Dad had some last minute errands to run so he was in town. Mum was finishing up with the packing with the help of friends.

At around 8pm we left for the airport. I said bye to Tina, and remembered how in the afternoon Perusy had given me one last massage as she gave Tina and I a pep talk on how to be ladies of integrity and dignity. She told us to respect our bodies so that men can also respect us. As I told Tina bye, I reminded her about that talk. We smiled and promised to give heed to that talk.

Off to the airport, I got into the boy's car with Steven, Evarist and Chaya, while Dad and Mum got into a different one. It was a nice ride to the airport. I looked out of the car window at the dim disappearing night lights which seemed to be a long stretched streak of light. When we got there Chaya held my hand and assisted me through the crowds. I told him to ring up some of my friends to let them know of my sudden trip. We found a spot where we all stood as we waited for the checking-in to start. We talked about how I would be back in a few weeks at most.

Finally, the time came for us to check in. I embraced all my brothers and then went in with Mum and Dad. They all told me to drop them an email as soon as I could see. It was an emotional moment. Part of me didn't want to leave but I had to for my own good. Dad asked the security guard to allow him in so that he could help us check in due to my inability to carry the luggage. He was granted permission. We went to the queue and the luggage was checked in. We then headed to the passport control department. After all was done, it came to the most emotional moment of all, telling my Daddy bye. He had been holding my hand the whole time. I did not want to let him go. He made a call to one Pr. Ngusa, who had been of great help through prayer. He prayed for us as we listened. He then wished us a safe trip. Then Dad prayed too, and then embraced Mum and me for a long time. I couldn't help but shed a few tears. I was really going to miss him. He had been with Mum and me from the beginning of the incident. It would be so different not having him around. I imagined how lonely he would be at home since Mum wouldn't be there. Evarist was headed back to school, too. Raphael would leave soon after. He was being subjected to life as a bachelor, a phase which he had let go of many years back. Who was going to help him choose what to wear or monitor his special diet or adjust his tie? The more I thought of this the more I cried. He then held my head between his hands as he wiped my tears and lovingly said,

"My dear, you are going to see again. Don't cry. God has already heard our prayers."

If only he knew I was crying for him, not me.

Mum and I then went to the waiting lounge. I strained to look around the room but Mum told me to stop hurting myself since my eyes were already red from crying. The time came for us to board the plane. They announced that children, the aged and the sick people were to board first. I fell into this category. One of the security officers helped me to the plane door, then Mum took over. She guided me through the aisle, being careful I did not bump into other passengers. We had been put in two separate seats so Mum requested one passenger if he could exchange seats and let us sit together. He refused.

On seeing this, a certain couple gave up their seats for our seats to let Mum and I sit together. We were very grateful to them. The plane was motionless on the runway for about twenty minutes or so. The flight attendants strolled up and down the aisle making sure that passengers had fastened their seatbelts and put bags in the overhead lockers. Mum had made sure mine was fastened. She gave Dad one last ring and I felt the tears well up again as I said one final farewell. Mum then whispered a prayer before the plane took off. I prayed that the next time I would be in that airport I would be able to see.

The journey to Amsterdam took approximately 8 hours; it was going to be a long flight. I felt so bad because I wasn't going to watch TV that whole time. I just stared blankly, straining to see the little screen in front of me. I put on the headphones to listen to the radio before sleeping and waking up during the meals or to be escorted to the bathroom. Mum never sleeps during flights so she read her Bible and Bible Study guide that she had not read since I had become sick. She had a lot of catching up to do.

We arrived at Schiphol airport, Amsterdam at the break of dawn. It was quite chilly so we had to grab some hot chocolate as we waited for our connecting flight to Detroit. Mum held my hand as we skirted through the duty-free shops. I had been there before but everything seemed all blurry, with a slight hint of light here and there. I could smell the different brands of fragrances and knew we were at the perfume shops. When I smelt the coffee and sandwiches I knew we were at the food court. I could also hear the announcements calling for passengers to board. I asked Mum how the outside was. She told me it was drizzling and there were so many planes outside and different airport vans, and fire trucks going in different directions on the runways. After our drinks, we called Dad. He and Evarist had just arrived in Mwanza that Saturday morning. We told them we were ok thus far. They wished us a safe journey for the remaining part.

After a while, we boarded the plane to Detroit. Flanking us were two gentlemen, both Americans, from their accent. I was reaching for my jacket when the man next to me said,

"If you are feeling cold here then I wonder what you will do in Detroit. My wife tells me the temperatures are in the negative."

"Oh my God! Then maybe I should get off this plane and go back home. I'll freeze!" I replied.

He laughed and replied,

"Don't worry, as long as you've got warm clothes you should be fine."

"I hope I do," I answered.

The man who sat next to Mum was a very talkative fellow; he was an army pilot. He told her about the times he had visited Africa. They talked almost the whole way. Mum told him the reason for our visit and he empathized with us. He gave us his contact details and told us to get in touch with him in case we ran into any problem. We were thankful, as he helped remove our luggage from the overhead locker when we landed at Detroit Airport.

Detroit airport was as cold as I had been warned, the coldest it had ever been in my life. It was snowing outside. My first snowfall and I couldn't see it, so Mum tried to explain how the soft white lumps fell and hit the ground like balls of cotton out in a field. The security check was menacingly long; it lasted almost an hour and a half. They opened all our suitcases and messed up our things and when they were done they just threw the things back in. It was very rude. I felt bad for Mum for she had spent the last couple of days neatly packing our bags and she would have to do it all over again.

We were interrogated about the purpose of our visit. We had to show proof of the doctor's letter and I could feel their cold stares turn sympathetic when they saw how genuine my case was. By the time we got to the waiting lounge we only had a couple of minutes before boarding the next plane to Baltimore, Maryland to my Aunt Anna's place. After boarding the plane, the flight was delayed due to the heavy snowfall. I tried to look out of the window; I could see it was all white. I strained to see the snow fall itself but I couldn't. We took off after a considerable wait, and before I had properly fallen asleep, we were landing at Baltimore Airport. It seemed to be full for I could feel the large masses of people rushing in different directions. As Mum guided me to the conveyer belt for our luggage I heard someone scream my name out and before I knew it she was hugging me. It was my aunt; Anna. She began crying as she embraced me tightly.

She hugged Mum, too, who told her not to cry for I was going to be fine. My aunt is usually very emotional so no matter how strong she was trying to be the tears seemed to overwhelm her. After she had composed herself, she took me to her car and turned on the heater because it was freezing outside. My uncle, Peter was there too; he was so happy to see me. My aunt went back to assist Mum with the luggage. They soon came back and we drove off to my aunt's place. There I was in USA, but I could not behold its beauty no matter how much I strained to look out the window.

When we got to her place, she gave me another sweater and coat to shield me from the cold. She then guided me down a couple of steps to the living room. The fire place was lit but it took time before I absorbed the heat. Ironically, not long before I would do anything to be under an air conditioner. Now the thought of it made me shiver inside. As I familiarized myself with the new place, I could tell it was cozy and homely from the cushions where I was sitting, the warm fireplace and the aroma of authentic cuisine that came from somewhere in the kitchen. Aunt Anna lived with a family from South Africa; they were temporary tenants. They had prepared dinner for us. Later, my aunt's eldest daughter, Ruth, came with her son Baraka. I hadn't seen her in a long time and as for Baraka I had never seen him before. I tried not to look at him in case I scared him off with my chameleon eyes.

Dinner was filled with laughter as people caught up on lost times. I was really tired so after a few yawns Aunt Anna took me to her bedroom to sleep. Since I was in an unfamiliar place, I could not sleep well, on top of that there was the jetlag since back home people were waking up to a new day. I eventually fell asleep looking forward to the next day.

Me and Lucky during the Youth conference in Taiwan

Dad sitting outside Muhimbili deep in thought. It was one of the last moments I witnessed before I went blind.

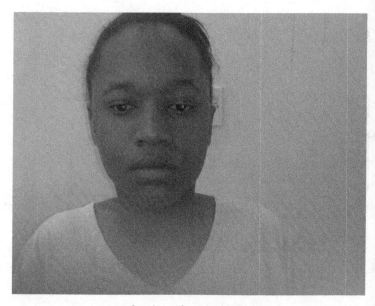

Me, a few days after I had gone blind

Lucky, Raph, Dad,Evarist,Mum, (In front) and me in the ward
at Hope Hospital

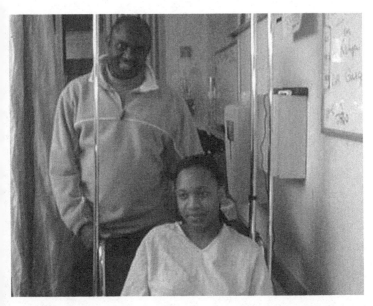

Uncle Peter and me before being wheeled off to the theatre
for the first surgery

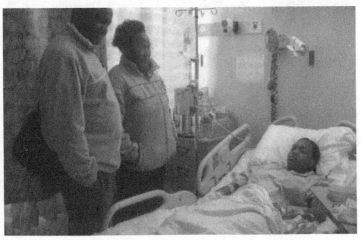

Uncle Peter and Mum talking to me after the surgery

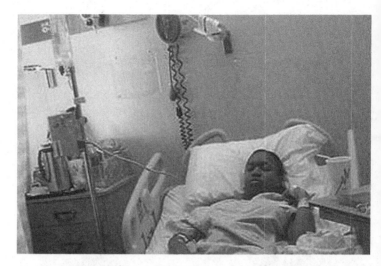

Me lying in UMass Memorial Hospital

Me & Mum enjoying the snow a few weeks after being
discharged from the hospital

Me, Aunt Anna & Uncle Peter outside the SDA General Conference in Washington

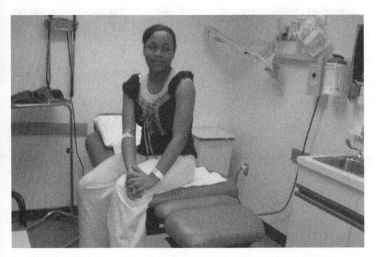

After being told I was being re-admitted, still in a state of disbelief

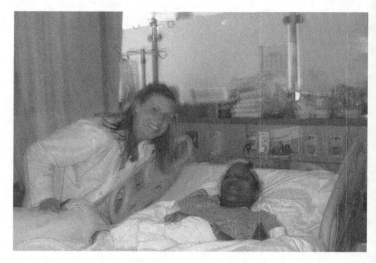

Dr. Julie & I just before surgery

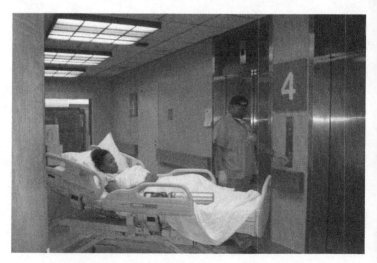

Me being wheeled off to surgery a second time

Mum in the waiting room. She's not smiling, just showing her teeth; she was anxious on the inside

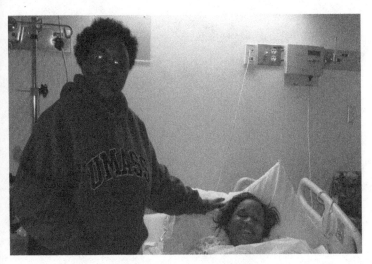

Mum & I at UMASS hospital

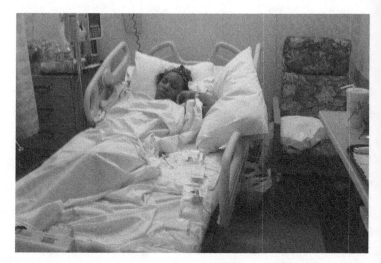

Me lying in UMASS

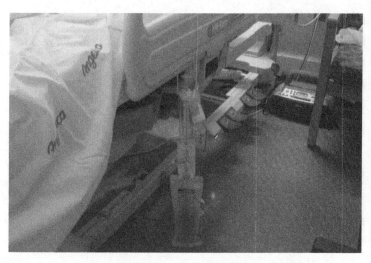

The catheter draining the excess spinal fluid

Me & Dad the day I saw him at Mwl. J.K Nyerere Airport
after 3 months apart

Dad, ,me and Dr. Annette during my third consultation in Dec 2008

Me at the Tribal Instinct charity fashion show event held
at the univeristy

Part Three

Finally morning came, Sunday, 27 January. After taking a hot shower I was guided to the dining area to have my breakfast. After that we called Violet; Ken's elder sister who had been informed of our visit and was expecting our call. After receiving directions to my aunt's place, she promised to come. In no time she was there. She greeted us like we knew each other. She embraced me like a long lost sister. I tried to study her face, but I could not see it clearly. Mum later tried to describe her to me, she looked like Ken but was fair skinned and had a beauty gap which was revealed whenever she talked or smiled. She was slightly plump and of medium height. I really wished I could see her, for she seemed like a wonderful person to be around. From her voice I could tell she was a charming person. Her laugh resounded in the room when she called Ken to tell him that she had fulfilled her promise of coming to see us. She asked about my sickness. As I narrated it to her as much as I could, she told me not to worry for God would fight for me.

After being with Violet for a while, Uncle Peter, Mum, Casmille, my uncle's friend and I bid her farewell because we had a long drive ahead of us to Massachusetts where Uncle Peter lives. The drive was approximately 8 hours. I tried to behold the alien land but it was in vain. I wanted to see the American sky, the skyscrapers as we passed by New York, the highways, the famous bridges, even the inter-state toll booths. Eventually, I gave up when all I saw was never ending shades of grey, green and once in a while more vibrant colours when a car or two overtook us. I decided to sleep so that I wouldn't feel like I was missing out on the beautiful scenery. We arrived in Leominster, Massachusetts at around 8pm. I was so tired from such a long drive and also the jetlag had not worn off. When I stepped out of the car, I stepped on what felt like a soft powdery substance-snow! I was so excited, I even removed my gloves to touch it, it was so cold and it melted after a while. I really wished I could see it. I brought it close to my eyes to have a closer look, but I wasn't successful. I was still excited since I had a bet with Lucky

61

to see who would see the snow first. Well I didn't see it but at least I touched it. I was so sure he would dispute saying it didn't count since I did not see it.

One of my uncle's friends, Virginia and her daughter, Yvonne, were there to welcome us. They greeted us cheerfully. They seemed really friendly. I couldn't see them well but I could tell they were nice by the way they spoke. Aunt Virginia had prepared some pilau rice, beef stew and chapatti for us. It smelled delicious, but I was not hungry. I was forced to eat though. As I ate, I tried to look around the house but I couldn't tell much. We sat at the dining table which was pushed to the wall so could only accommodate four people, and there were some couches, I didn't know how many at first. There was a TV; I could hear a comedy show was on. Although Yvonne seemed to be my age, we did not say more than two words to each other. I avoided eye contact with people I had just met, for fear of making them uncomfortable with my blank stares. I either looked down most of the time or just closed my eyes.

After dinner another one of my uncle's friends, Jamal, came too. He and Mum seemed to know each from our hometown. Laughter resounded in the room, as the adults shared some jokes, while Yvonne sat watching TV and I sat on the couch with my eyes closed. I was jealous that she got to watch TV and I just listened to voices from the TV. I tried to put a face to the different characters, whether I was right I would never know since I don't remember what program it was. After a few minutes, we left Yvonne behind and got into the car and headed to the hospital almost half an hour away. When we got to the hospital, I was taken straight to the emergency department and registered, then I was taken to another room to wait for a doctor. It was a very cold night so I requested for more blankets. The doctor arrived shortly and after greeting us, she asked me to explain what had happened. I narrated the now memorized tale. She then requested me to open my eyes wide as she looked into my eye with a torch. I did not blink the whole time. I could hear Aunt Virginia whisper to Mum how the bright light did not make me flinch even a bit. Mum just whispered back saying that was how real the situation was. After observing my non-responsive eyes for a while, the doctor requested a nurse to check my vital signs - blood pressure and temperature. After which I was wheeled into what seemed like a bigger and more equipped room. The doctor told me that in a few minutes someone from the laboratory would come to draw some blood for further tests. She left shortly after, I looked around the room. I could tell Mum was sitting closest to me. As for Uncle Peter, Jamal and Aunt Virginia, I was not sure where they stood although I could hear their mumbled conversations somewhere in the room. Someone came to draw blood; he came back several times since he said he needed a lot of blood to carry out different tests.

Other specialists came as well; neurosurgeons, neurologists, ophthalmologists, hematologists, cardiologists and many more. It was as though every part of my body was being tested. They all came at different intervals, and I could not see them properly no matter how much I tried to study their faces. They all carried different tests. Hematologists drew blood samples, neurosurgeons requested for an MRI that was carried out that very night, ophthalmologists used different equipment to look into my eyes and eye drops to dilate my pupils and measure the eye pressure and called each other to have a look and explain what they saw. For the entire night they kept coming and going; they would wake me up when they found me asleep and apologize before carrying out further tests.

Uncle Peter, Jamal, and Aunt Virginia took turns sleeping as they had work the next day. Mum and Aunt Virginia are tea lovers, so they kept drinking tea throughout the night. By morning all necessary tests had been carried out since fewer doctors came into the room. The other three except Mum left, but promised to be back later.

The hematologist came in with the blood test results. After the usual morning courtesies, he quipped,

"Margareth, the tests show that you are very anemic. Did you know about this?"

"Yes, doctor." I answered.

63

He went on to say,

"It is chronic. Your HB level is very low. We need to carry out some more tests so as to determine the cause."

"How much blood will be drawn for the tests since there might not be any left?" I said this in a jocular tone.

"Just enough to determine the cause. Don't worry, we will spare you some," he replied reassuringly.

He finished saying this as the neurologists walked in with the results of the MRI scans. After greeting us, they said,

"There seems to be a problem with the optic nerve. It appears a bit swollen and inflamed. Thus we have to check your cerebral fluid pressure."

"How do you check it?" I inquired.

"We draw some fluid from the end of your spine using a syringe."

"Is it painful?" I was scared.

"From what other patients say, I would say it depends on the individual. Some say it is, while others say it is not."

"But it can't be too painful, right?" I asked hoping she would reassure me.

"No, I don't think so. We inject some anesthesia around the region, so you have to be very still."

"Okay, so when will you carry it out?"

"As soon as you sign these papers we will be back with the equipment and get started."

"Can my mum sign on my behalf since I can't see the writing?"

"Yes, she can as long as you have chosen her to be your guarantor."

"Yes, I have. She can sign."

So Mum signed and the doctor left the room. One of the first things I noticed that was so different from our hospitals back home, apart from the equipment and technology, was the extra hospitality of the nurses and doctors. A nurse would come at random times and ask if I needed anything. He or she would say things like, "Honey do you need anything" or "Hey dear, you will be fine" or "Hi darling, I would like to draw some blood." And so on and so forth. As a patient lying there I would feel better just from their soft and caring tones. Even while drawing the blood it seemed less painful. I don't mean to say that the nurses at home are horrible, not at all. It is just that the ones here seemed more sympathetic and warm towards patients.

The neurologist, Dr. Gaag, a gentle, caring young lady of Chinese descent as Mum described to me later, came to perform the simple but delicate procedure. I was asked to curl up on my left side like a kidney and stay still for a few minutes, a slight shift would have been disastrous to the whole procedure. I stayed as calm as I could. My eyes squinted as the needle pierced through to my spine. As the doctor drew out the fluid, Mum commented;

"I never knew that there is such clear fluid in our bodies."

"Is it so clear?" I asked

"Yes, it is so clear and pure almost like water from a spring or rain water that collects on the roof gutter."

That analogy made me visualize the clarity of the fluid. As the doctor had promised me that the procedure lasted only a short while. It was not painful at all, apart from the initial pinch as the syringe prodded into my back. She told us the results would be ready later in the day and then she left.

The ophthalmologists came to have a look at my eyes again. They said that my eyes appeared pale and that the optic discs were serrated. Also the optic nerve appeared to be pale pink instead of bright red. This was similar to what Dr. Bowman had diagnosed.

Later in the day the neurosurgeon, Dr. Julie came.

"Margareth, after going through all the tests we have discovered that your cerebral fluid is in excess so it creates an elevated intracranial pressure in the brain. This caused the optic nerve to swell, therefore distorting the light from getting into your eyes. This is also the reason for the constant headaches. Your condition is commonly known as pseudotumor cerebri, which is a rare condition found predominantly in obese women of childbearing age. It's a bit puzzling since you don't fall into that category."

"Wow, this is all a bit too much to take in at once, doctor," I told her as I turned to Mum whom I could tell was deep in thought.

"I know," she politely said. "So we are moving you to the wards for admission. We have already put you on the waiting list for surgery on Wednesday, 30 January. I know this will take a while to sink in, but for now we have to carry out the operation as soon as possible."

"Doctor, what may have triggered this condition?" I inquired after a short silence.

"There isn't a specific cause or trigger. It rarely occurs, too."

"Forgive me for all the questions, but please explain to me how the operation will be carried out"

"I will explain everything in detail tomorrow as we prepare you for the surgery on Wednesday. Do you have any more questions?"

I shook my head and with that she excused herself and left the room.

I sat in the room with Mum as she prayed, thanking God that the problem had at last been identified. She called Uncle Peter to tell him what the doctor had said. He was also happy that I was finally going to begin treatment. Mum played with my fingers as we waited to be transferred to the ward. I asked her if I could see her hands; she stretched them for me but I couldn't see her supple arms that always held me so dearly. I told her that I would soon be able to see them. Lucky and I always played with her arms and even competed to be held by them until Mum would chase us away and tell us to leave her alone, jokingly of course.

Later I was taken up to the 4th floor of UMass Memorial Hospital where all neurological cases were dealt with. The room seemed big and spacious; it was for two people. The bed was self-sufficient, it had a remote control for the TV which was useless to me but helpful for the visitors, a lever to move it up and down; it could give a massage with the push of a button; it had a phone; and a nurse's call button too. I felt for all these devices so that I knew exactly where they were in case I needed them. Mum later told me there were also some gas tanks in case I ever needed some extra oxygen. There was one visitor's seat where Mum sat as we familiarized ourselves with the new place. My uncle came in the evening and stayed for a while before he left. Both doctors and nurses came to attend to me. Blood was being drawn almost every hour.

Later that evening Aunt Virginia's eldest daughter, Monique, came. She was a very easy person to talk to. She could strike up a conversation easily. She even brought me her iPod to listen to while at the hospital. She made sure she had set it on 'All songs' so that I didn't struggle looking for tracks on my own. She barely knew me but she treated me as if we knew each other. She reminded me of Tina, not by the way she spoke, but by her actions. I tried to make out her face but it was too difficult. She stayed there until late, and then she left with Mum. The hospital did not allow overnight visitors. I was left alone; it was the first time since I had become sick that I slept alone in the hospital. At first I was scared of being left alone with total strangers who I couldn't even see, but then I relaxed and fell asleep. I slept soundly, only to be woken up by nurses who wanted to take my vital signs. The nurses would ask if I needed anything to drink. I told them no thanks for I was too sleepy to drink anything. When I asked for the time, they told me it was around 4am. I fell asleep as soon as they left.

Tuesday, January 29, Dr. Julie and Dr. Jeff, her colleague, came. Actually Jeff came in first to explain how the procedure was going to be carried out. He said,

"We are going to drill a hole from the top of the skull then insert a tube that goes through the back of your neck to the end of the spine. This will help drain out the excess fluid from your brain." He said this with an authoritative tone indicating finality.

I was perturbed, my body was shaking, my face felt hot. I felt my eyes fill up with tears. Before the tears overwhelmed me, I managed to ask,

"Is there no other way that does not involve drilling through my skull?"

"There is, but I have decided to go with this one. It's my speciality," he replied with a tone that I felt was a bit mocking.

He left after he said this. I felt numb. I began thinking of the whole procedure. I could imagine them drilling through my skull, it felt like a nightmare which no matter how much I tried to wake up from it, I couldn't. My stomach churned at the thought of a drill. I envisioned the scar that would be left along the path of the operation that would trigger so many questions later in life. Mum tried rubbing my back in the hope of calming me down. I wasn't enthusiastic when some of my uncle's friends came to visit me. Mum explained to them what the doctor had said so they wouldn't be offended since it was the first time they were meeting me.

When the nurse came to take my vitals, she gasped at how drastically my blood pressure had risen, thus she had to get Dr. Julie to have a look at me. The doctor told me it was because I was so shocked on receiving the news, but it would eventually fall back to normal. She went on to say,

"Margareth, we have decided to change the procedure since we have seen how affected you were by the other one." She said this with a light note.

"That's good to hear. I hope it does not involve drilling."

"No drilling." I could sense a smile as she said this, "We are going to put a Lumbar Peritoneal (LP) Shunt from the end of your spine round through the left side and it will end near the belly button region where it will drain the excess fluid into the normal digestive tract."

She paused as though to let me absorb the chunky information she had just dropped on me. I sighed heavily, obviously relieved. Then she asked;

"Do you have any questions?"

"Yes, doctor, approximately how long is the procedure likely to take?"

"About two hours at most. It is not such a long procedure." She replied, quite confident in herself.

"Does the shunt stay with me all my life or is it removed after a while?"

"Unfortunately, it stays. Because we do not know how the excess fluid comes about and it won't stop, the shunt has to stay in order to always drain it out." I could feel sympathy in her voice.

Then with great concern I asked the million dollar question, "Will I be able to see after the surgery?"

She had been expecting this question for sure. She was silent for a moment before she softly replied,

"I'm afraid we cannot guarantee that your sight will come back," she paused, letting me swallow that bitter expert truth or opinion. "Because, Maggie, the damage is great as it is. So I cannot guarantee whether the nerve will recuperate. We hope it will though."

She wished she could give me better news than that but her expertise told her otherwise. After an uncomfortable silence, I confidently said,

"I will see again, doctor, I know I will." Whether it was the fear of blindness that gave me such confidence or the thought of so many people praying for me, I knew I would see again.

"Well, that is great if you believe so. It is good to be optimistic," she replied as though wondering if I hadn't heard what she had said about there being great damage that might not recover.

To me, I believed in God who is greater than my big problem, the One who created the heavens and the earth, the God who formed me in my mother's womb, the One who divided the Red Sea to let his people walk on dry land, the One who opened up the earth so it would swallow the disobedient, the God who raised the dead, the One who gave sight to the blind Bartimaeus. That was the God I served and nothing was ever too hard for Him to handle.

She then left and soon after the anesthesiologist came to explain how the anesthesia would work. He asked me if I was allergic to any kind of medication. I told him there were none that I knew of. He went on to explain how they would first induce some anesthesia in my Intravenous (IV) tube, which had been injected in my right hand so that they could draw blood anytime before being wheeled off to the theatre, followed by the one that would knock me out completely for the entire procedure.

He then warned me not to eat anything past midnight that day. I asked for the reason and he told me it was to prevent the anesthesia from reacting with the food which could affect my bowel movement. After he was done, he told me he would see me the next day.

The rest of the day was filled with visitors who brought me some home-cooked meals that were very appetizing. When my uncle came from work Mum told him everything the doctors had said, including the surgery time, which was scheduled for 11am the following day. Mum also called Dad to inform him of the events of the next day. I talked to him and he reassured me that everything was going to be fine and that I should not be afraid of the surgery for I would get through it well. It was as though he had sensed my fear. Honestly, I was a bit scared of the operation. I had so many questions; what if I didn't wake up from the operating table? What if something went wrong during the procedure? What if the anesthesia wore off before the procedure was done? Such fears I kept to myself because I knew Mum would rebuke such thoughts if I told her. She called a few more people to tell them to pray for my prospective surgery. Some promised to fast and pray specifically for that matter.

Aunt Virginia and her sister aunt Lydia came to see me in the evening. When Mum told them what the doctors had said, aunt Lydia led us in a very powerful prayer. I couldn't wait to see all the wonderful people who came to visit me at the hospital. Aunt Lydia was just as humorous and caring as her sister. They filled the room with throaty laughter as they tried to ease my anxiety.

After everyone had left, I prayed, too, for God to help me get through the operation well and that I would see again. I also prayed for peace of mind. It was a long night. I kept waking up thinking morning had come. Whether I opened my eyes or closed them it made no difference, the room just looked dark and scary. The gentle snore of my roommate made it less scary since I knew there was someone else in the room. I could hear some other patients call for the nurses to adjust a thing or two. I could hear the nurses scuffling through the corridors as they attended to these patients. There were so many beeping noises that came from neighbouring rooms; probably their IVs or heart monitors. Eventually I fell asleep.

Morning finally came, on Wednesday, 30 January. The nurse woke me up to check on my vital signs. She asked me if I was nervous about the surgery. I told her a little. She said,

"Don't worry honey, you'll be fine."

The sweet aroma of my roommate's breakfast reminded me that I couldn't eat. With that thought in mind, my stomach grumbled at the torture it was being subjected to. My roommate I could tell was Indian from the way she spoke. She groaned in pain and kept asking for ice to cool off her hand for she felt it was on fire; it was broken. It was typical for such accidents to occur during the winter due to slippery, icy roads. I wished I could help her get the ice for she seemed to be in excruciating pain but I could hardly help myself.

Mum came with Monique. The latter had a camera to take some photos to remind me of that day and so that I would see how the room looked and Monique herself when my sight returned. It is a day that will be etched in my mind forever since it is the day I received my first surgery. We prayed before leaving the room for the theatre.

The nurse then wheeled me off to the waiting room with Mum and Monique following closely behind. Other nurses took over and they prepared me for surgery. They cross checked my details on the confirmation sheet Mum had signed permitting them to carry out the surgery. After that the anesthesia team came to conduct their very vital procedure. Mum prayed again as she held my hand dearly as though she did not want to let me go. I promised her that I would pull through. As I was still talking, I felt my speech begin to slur, then felt my body grow numb and then… then I was gone.

During the time I had passed out, Mum later told me what transpired. She waited in the lounge with Monique who later left and was replaced by Uncle Peter. Mum said as she sat in the lounge she kept praying that everything would go well. She couldn't eat since she had lost all appetite due to being anxious. As she sat with my uncle, suddenly Dr. Jeff approached them with a worried expression. Her heart skipped a beat for I had only been in the theatre for half an hour, what could possibly have gone wrong?

No sooner had she begun to walk briskly up the stairs towards the doctor than Dr. Julie also appeared. She felt her legs grow weak and give way. She just sat at the stairs fearing the worst. She told my uncle to talk to them for she did not have the strength to hear what they had to say. The doctor approached them and quickly asked,

"I'm sorry I forgot to ask whether your daughter was pregnant before administering the anesthesia."

"She is not pregnant" he replied with almost obvious relief.

Mum went on to anxiously ask,

"But is everything ok? Is she doing well?"

The doctor could tell Mum had been deeply affected by the sight of the two doctors so she reassuringly replied,

"She is doing fine. It was our fault we had forgotten to ask earlier. I have to get back now. I will keep you posted on her progress; excuse me."

With that both doctors rushed off to the operating room. Uncle Peter, who had also been slightly shaken let out a sigh. He helped Mum to climb up the remaining stairs and they sat in the lounge, talking silently before Aunt Virginia joined them. Mum told her about the slight scare. That whole time I lay unconscious in the theatre not knowing what was happening either in the world of the living or the dead.

The next thing I knew I could hear people talking from a distance. My eyelids were heavy and drowsy. I tried opening them as much as I could, but the forces pulling them together seemed stronger, it was a losing battle so I kept my eyes shut. My throat felt very dry and sore. My breathing felt confined and I slowly became aware that I was breathing through an oxygen face mask. I tried opening my eyes again, I felt disoriented in my own pitch-darkness even though the room I was in was full of machine bleeps and movement. I wondered where I was.

Someone came and from a distance I heard her ask,

"Honey, are you awake?"

I just mumbled a reply and lazily nodded, since my whole body felt a kind of deadly fatigue, as though I was swimming through a pool of tar. When I mustered up some energy I asked,

"Where am I?"

"You are in a recovery room dear," she gently replied, her voice sounding so distant, "your surgery went very well."

"Where's my mum?" I asked realizing I had not heard her warm voice near me.

"She's in the waiting room. She will meet you in the ward," she assured me.

I tried to ask something else, before she warned me,

"Don't strain yourself darling, just rest."

Shortly after, I felt myself being wheeled along and in a few minutes I had entered my room. Mum greeted me with great enthusiasm and I smiled weakly.

"Your procedure took longer than expected, and we were worried. Glory is to God that you're okay", she remarked thankfully. Then, Aunt Virginia greeted me as well. As usual Uncle Peter greeted me with jokes. I resisted laughing for my throat hurt.

As the anesthesia wore off, I began regaining my sense of feeling; from my back along the left side and on to my belly I was wrapped in fresh bandages. Mum asked me if I was in any pain. I candidly answered her that I didn't feel any at the time. She tried to feed me some mashed potatoes and chicken gravy ignoring my lack of appetite. When the anesthesia wore off completely, I felt some slight pain and a minor headache. I was given an analgesic pill then I was told to rest.

Thursday, January 31, I woke up feeling weary. My head was pounding spasmodically. I felt as though I was out of breath and was gasping for air. The room felt like it lacked adequate ventilation. I tried opening my eyes but they were too heavy and weak. I tried lifting my hand but I could barely lift a finger, my body had lost all its energy. The only sound I managed to make so as to get some attention was a painful groan. For a moment I felt as though the stealthy hands of death were approaching slowly and getting closer and closer to strangle me around the neck. I was too weak to fight back; I felt nauseated. All this time, Mum was by my side not knowing what to do as I writhed in bed having pain that she couldn't take away. She had called a nurse who had given me a morphine pill to alleviate the pain but it did not seem to work. I weakly asked for more pills but was denied since not enough time had elapsed since the last dose.

I barely ate that morning; my mouth felt bitter but Mum somehow managed to force some mashed potatoes and gravy down my throat. When Dr. Julie came to check on my progress, I could tell she was worried. She left and returned with the hematologist. He told Mum I needed a blood transfusion since my blood was very low. Mum said she needed time to consult Uncle Peter and Dad before giving her consent.

"I'm sorry ma'am but there is no time for consultation. You need to make this decision fast because her life is in danger due to lack of blood," he implored anxiously.

She paused for a moment before allowing them to proceed seeing how critical my condition was.

The blood had to be brought from the bank then tested before being transfused into my deficient body. This happened late in the evening. I mumbled a prayer to God as I struggled to fight for my life. Tears flowed freely as I lay in bed waiting for the transfusion. Mum dabbed them off my face and held my hand telling me to hang in there. Uncle Peter finally came. He was very disturbed at the sight of me lying there helpless. Coincidentally, Dad called at that very moment. Mum disguised her worry as she talked to him. She knew if she told him how critical my condition was and he was thousands of miles away he would be devastated that he couldn't be by my bedside when I needed him. He would panic if he knew the truth then. When Dad asked to talk to me Mum told him that I was resting.

I wondered whether I would make it through the night. I was tempted to tell Mum to pack our belongings and leave the hospital to catch the next flight back home so I would rest in peace there. I did not want the worst to happen where Mum would have to travel on her own back home, and pay freight fees for the casket holding my remains that held no value. Unfortunately, I was too weak to relay all these thoughts to her. I held her hand gently, caressing it to and fro. I tried to look at her face, at least one last time. I couldn't see it so I knew that I needed to see it one last time before saying goodbye. I hung on to the last threads of my life determined to make it. Mum didn't return to my uncle's place that evening. She requested to stay with me and this was granted. The nurses had seen how grave my condition was so it was only reasonable to let her stay.

In the midst of my pain and struggle, a nurse finally came. I heard her setting up the intravenous drip and then reach for my right hand and gently insert a needle. I squinted at the initial prick. From time to time Mum would hold my free hand just to let me know she was still by my side. She hardly slept a wink that night. As the solution in the intravenous drip slowly flowed into my bloodstream, I managed to doze off as the pain eased out.

Early the next morning, Friday, February 1st, Mum came to see how I was getting on since at some point in the night she had left to lie down in the visitors lounge. She found me sound asleep, clearly responding to the treatment. She didn't wake me up, but sat by my bed side and read her Bible. She occasionally threw a glance at me as I rested peacefully, breathing slowly. Uncle Peter rushed into my room also to see how I was fairing for he had also been slightly shaken by my state the previous day. He was relieved to see me lying there peacefully, not writhing, not in pain, just resting. He left for work without waking me up, for his mind was at ease. I eventually woke up struggling to open my heavy eyes. I darted them round the room searching for Mum. I tried to lift my hand which I managed with so much ease. I called out for Mum and turned to the direction her voice came from and greeted her.

As she gave me breakfast which I ate hungrily, I asked her about the transfusion.

"First, they gave you iron and then a pint of blood. You are still on your first bag, sweetheart," she explained as she stuffed me with soup.

"How much blood am I going to be given?" I asked turning to look at the IV drip towering over my bed.

"Just two pints. You should be done by noon," she answered with gladness in her voice.

Even the doctors were impressed to see that I had improved. After my breakfast I went back to sleep only to wake up later when I had visitors. They were glad that I appeared cheerful. They wished me a quick recovery. Uncle Peter came in later with a radio so that I wouldn't be too bored during the night. Monique also brought me some more music. That evening, I received more visitors since it was already the weekend, hence more people were free. When it was time to leave, they all left including Mum; she was confident I was fine. I thanked God for seeing me through that day and the previous one. I fell asleep to the soothing country music from the radio.

Saturday came. I was glad it was the weekend so my uncle didn't have to go to work and could spend the whole day at the hospital with Mum and me. We talked and laughed, sang and prayed. It was a blessed Sabbath day even though it was spent in hospital. More visitors came and left. That day I felt that the pain had subsided. I didn't moan for the morphine as I had before. The rest of the weekend went by smoothly. I was being discharged on Monday. Dr. Julie booked me an appointment after six weeks. The hematologist prescribed some iron pills to take for a month. Dr. Gaag gave me an appointment after two weeks.

My uncle could not make it so he sent Aunt Virginia to pick us up from the hospital. I woke up with a pounding headache, my body was weak too. Before being discharged, I had to see my Primary Care Physician who told me it was just the after effects of the surgery and that it would eventually get better. She also told me to maintain a horizontal position thus I was to lie down most of the time in order for the pressure to slowly decrease. She prescribed me some morphine and Tylenol to help alleviate the pain.

Then Aunt Virginia wheeled me out to her awaiting car as Mum followed closely. It was raining and very cold. I had been so used to the warmth in my hospital room that I had forgotten the reality of the bitter winter outside. I slept in the back seat through the whole drive back to my uncle's place. My head was still throbbing so I never said a word to anyone.

When we arrived home, I slept most of the afternoon and only woke up when I was forced to eat. Uncle Peter came home and was glad to find us there. Soon after dinner I retired to bed again. I hugged the warm comforter and slept on my back or my right side careful not to injure my still fresh incisions.

The next day Monique was leaving for Brazil for a school exchange program. She came to say bye and we took some photos so that I would put a face to her voice once my sight returned. I was not sure I was going to meet her again since she would be gone for a while and I would probably have left by the time she came back. I felt sad since she was the only age mate I had really bonded with.

The rest of the week just flew by with the same routine: waking up, taking a bath, eating, sleeping on the sofa as I listened to different TV programs, especially the courtroom dramas. During those shows I would tell Mum who I thought was guilty from the debates I heard. She just chuckled and told me she was happy I was still determined to pursue the legal career. I also reflected on Dr. Bwana's statement about the blind Lord Justice. It made sense why he would be so impartial, by not being able to see the parties in question, he would strictly base his judgment on the evidence and arguments presented rather than sympathizing with their appearances.

That Saturday we were invited for lunch at Geliga's place. He and his wife, Bahati, were my uncle's friends and also came from the same village as Mum. The lunch was like a banquet; so much variety to choose from. The afternoon was filled with laughter as they reminded each other of stories of life back home. I sat at the table with their son, Mateja, as the rest sat in the sitting area enjoying their meal. As I ate, I would miss my plate and eat from the table. Mateja giggled at this; I was slightly embarrassed since I had never met him before and he was around the same age as me. We didn't talk much, just exchanged a little random chat once in a while.

After he finished his meal, he went to his room as I was finishing my meal. Then as I attempted to make my way to the sitting room, my uncle rushed to my side to prevent me from clattering the objects that were placed around the room. They continued talking and laughing as I sat in my darkened world listening and laughing occasionally. The evening wore on and we eventually returned home.

Sunday, 10 February, I woke up unusually excited. I looked down at my fingernails. "I need to cut my nails," I thought as I studied them.

"I need to cut my nails!" I screamed. Had I just noticed my fingers? Had I just seen my nails? I jumped out of bed and carefully strode to the sitting room, the location of which I had already figured out during the past couple of days.

"Mum I can see my nails!" I quipped with joy, "I can even see my hand!"

"Praise God!" she cried out as she embraced me.

"Wow! That is great dear," Uncle Peter chimed in.

"What else can you see dear?" Mum asked, with obvious anticipation.

I looked at her face. I saw her beautiful smile which I had dearly missed.

"I can see your smile, Mama." I touched her face, it was like I was looking at it for the first time in months; it had been a month. I couldn't help but shed a small tear. I was glad. My vision had not cleared up completely but at least I could see someone whom I held so dearly, I could see that wonderful smile that was always reassuring me of her constant love. I embraced her again. Mum also couldn't help shedding a tear. She was thankful that I was better than I had been since my incident began.

My uncle also embraced me. He was also clearly relieved that there was some improvement. I then asked Mum for her phone.

"Why do you need it?" she asked as she handed it to me, not sure of my sudden interest.

"I want to see if I can see the screen and read the font." I replied excitedly as I stared at the screen. I could see the sky blue background and a hazy pink image that I couldn't make out. The letters appeared all huddled close together thus difficult to make out the words.

"No, I still can't see it," I said, sounding slightly disappointed.

"One day at a time honey. Don't push yourself. Just be thankful that you are making progress," Mum said encouragingly.

I smiled. She was right, one day at a time. This was still exciting. I asked her to call Dad for he had to be informed of the good news. And he was told everything. He told me to keep on believing that things will be fine. That whole day I saw my world from a different perspective; it was not pitch black any more, it was more of a thick grey cloud hanging round my field of view; a significant improvement.

Monday, February 11, I had an appointment with an ophthalmologist in Boston. Mum complained of some chest aches she was experiencing and also difficulty in breathing. On our way to my appointment, she said she was freezing even though she was wrapped in a duvet inside the car with the heating turned on. She was still shaking, Although she tried to be brave, the feverish feeling got the better of her. When we got to the hospital, she grabbed herself a cup of steaming hot tea to keep her warm.

As we sat there waiting to be called in, I asked Uncle Peter to describe for me the view from the window that faced us. We were up on the tenth floor. He told me of the different buildings that spread out all over the city. There was one distinct rounded glass building that towered above the rest in the middle, which seemed to be swallowed by the fog around it. There were so many highways intersecting at different angles; many underpasses and flyovers, different exits leading away from the city. Further away he could see the Logan International Airport next to the Atlantic Ocean. There was also a pretty deserted park since it was raining outside. There was a frozen pond in the middle of the park. He told me of how in the summer people would enjoy spending time in the parks. Some people rushed in different directions in the streets, tightly clutching their umbrellas and coats. His description of the scenery made me wish I could enjoy it myself, I tried but all that came into view was a series of vague images, but I could not pick out anything in particular.

I was soon called in. The ophthalmologist seemed to be a man advanced in age from the way he spoke. He greeted us firmly and asked me to sit down on a black variable-height couch. I sat on my own since I could indistinctly see it. He looked into my eyes with a small torch. For once I could see some light from the torch but I still didn't blink. He also put a liquid to dilate my pupils and also check for the eye pressure. He then sent me to the visual field room where they were to take a picture of the back of my eye and carry out some other tests. I was supposed to focus my eye on a certain red spot so that they could take the picture clearly. I couldn't see it so they kept telling me to shift my eyes until they were satisfied they could get a clear image. It was a long, strenuous exercise. I was also supposed to press a certain button whenever I saw a streak of light as I looked into the machine. For the whole five minutes I didn't press the button. There was just a hollow darkness. I returned to the ophthalmologist's office, and he was handed the test results. He asked me to read some letters from a chart stuck on a wall. I couldn't. He then asked me to count the fingers he held up. I couldn't do that either. He finally said in a matter of fact tone,

"From what I see, your eyes don't look good, so I will have you registered as legally blind so you can receive help from your local nurses. They will provide you with equipment to aid you and also counseling on how to adapt to your condition."

I burst into tears, I couldn't speak for a while. The term 'legally blind' had caught me off guard and I was overcome with emotion. My mind went back to the first day I had gone blind; the day when all hopes were washed away; the day when the cruel darkness had stolen my sight. It was painful hearing those words leave the doctor's lips. I felt weak and helpless. Amidst the tears I asked,

"So does this mean I won't ever see again?" I cried even more at the thought of it being a possibility.

"I'm not sure. Come back after three months, then we'll see. However, since the damage is so great, I have my doubts." As he said this, he booked me an appointment in three months' time.

I wept even more. He did not seem sympathetic at all. As we left his office, I continued crying. My uncle tried to calm me down. He told me that it didn't mean I wouldn't see again. That didn't stop me from crying. Mum, who had stayed out during my consultation, was surprised to see me sobbing. She asked me what had happened and when I couldn't answer she asked my uncle. He explained to her. She rubbed my back gently and told me exactly what my uncle had told me but added that God would see me through. I still cried. My uncle opted for a more professional help. He got hold of one of the doctors and told them what had happened then asked them to explain to me what the term 'legally blind' meant. He said,

"It's just that you are not able to see like normal people so you need assistance. It doesn't mean that you won't see again."

I stopped crying and I was trying to control the sniffles. I was still upset, not because I had just been declared legally blind, but because of the way the ophthalmologist had said it. It was harsh and slightly condemning.

The drive back home was a quiet one. Mum lay in the back seat trying to get a rest as she struggled to breathe and coughed spasmodically. I was deep in thought about what the doctor had just said. I feared the worst. Uncle Peter hummed to the CD playing. Occasionally he would whistle the tunes. The music lifted my spirits as we drove back home. By the time we got home, I was singing along the songs. Music is therapeutic and for sure it mended my broken spirit.

I even forgot how I had cried in the lounge back at the hospital. I had asked God,

"Am I really not going to see again? God, you know I have so many plans ahead of me. Are you really going to let me be blind for the rest of my life?"

I had cheered up but Mum was not well. She was still feeling feverish. She took some malaria tablets which she had carried from home thinking they would help relieve the malaria symptoms she felt. It wouldn't be surprising if it turned out to be malaria, having succumbed to the mosquitoes at Hope Hospital. The pills did not help. The symptoms persisted and even affected her sleep. She would wake up in the middle of the night and sit on the bed for a long time for she felt out of breath whenever she lay down. I felt sorry for her. I did not know how to help her. I secretly cried since I did not want her to suffer like that. She had already endured a lot nursing me that last month, yet alone bringing me up all those years. She was weak and had lost her appetite for food. By Friday she surrendered and we took her to the hospital; the same one as I had been admitted to, UMASS Memorial Hospital.

When we got to the hospital, she was rushed to the emergency room and was registered immediately. A nurse came to draw some blood for the lab tests and we waited for a doctor to attend to her. She was still shivering even though she had been provided with enough blankets and had also worn many layers of warm sweaters and a jacket. One could hear her breathe with difficulty as she lay on the bed. She was then wheeled off to have a chest x-ray.

My uncle and I took a walk in the emergency room as we waited for her to get back. I could feel the warm sunshine on my face as we neared the large windows. I could see its faint light filtered through the half-opened window as it shone dimly on my hazy eyes. I could also see the white snow on the ground below and a few cars as they drove past. From my perspective it seemed like a wintry evening with a distant sunset even though it was only 10am. I told my uncle my latest developments, and he was happy. I couldn't wait to tell Mum once she felt better.

We then went back to Mum's room in time to receive the test results. Mum was diagnosed with pneumonia and her blood count was low. The doctor advised her to drink a lot of fluids and have plenty of rest. She was prescribed antibiotics and we left shortly after she had taken her first dose. She fell asleep as soon as we got home. I kept checking up on her to see if she was alright. I was nursing her now.

Mum got progressively better over the weekend and during the following week. We got plenty of invites to people's homes and likewise they came to visit us as well. They prepared African dishes that reminded us of life back home. I met Lindiwe and her Mum, who had invited us one day. They had cooked so much that we were spoilt for choice. Lindiwe was very chatty and we bonded instantly. She and Yvonne also knew each other from school. I was glad to have people of my age to talk to.

One Saturday we went to church. That was the first time in a long while. From where we were sitting, I could neither see the altar nor the pastor, I just listened to the sermon as I maintained a forward gaze at what I assumed would be the altar. After the service people came to greet us. I just smiled back in greeting as I couldn't make out their faces but I could recognize some of their voices. Some stretched out their hands and I didn't see them until Mum whispered to me, and I searched to greet their outstretched hands

That evening, we had a dinner invite at Aunt Virginia's house. Aunt Lydia was there too. I met Daniel, Virginia's only son. Yvonne was not home when we arrived so I sat curled up on the couch covered in a duvet, as the three women drank their tea and laughed at something on the TV. I couldn't tell much from where I sat; I knew there was a TV next to where I was sitting since I could see the flashing colours of different images on the screen. There were three sofas and a small coffee table which had been moved away so that I wouldn't walk into it. I didn't go to the kitchen or the dining table, just to be on the safe side.

Yvonne came later with Lindiwe and Rehema, another of their friends, who spoke with a very soft, calm voice. We went up to

Yvonne's room so we could hang out as our mothers drank their tea downstairs. I tried to attach faces to their different voices as we talked and laughed, since I couldn't really see them clearly. I couldn't look at them closely for it would have freaked them out, I thought. So there I was talking to people of whom I had no idea how they looked like, but we made conversation as though we had been friends for a long time.

Later, Yvonne asked her mum if they could take me to meet some of their friends. She agreed and my mum conferred with her. While we were out, I felt out of place. I was shy since I couldn't see many people who were thronging around our table. Yvonne tried her best to include me in the conversations but it was hard since I couldn't make out people's faces. I tried to avoid gawking at people so my eyes darted around the room to avoid direct eye contact with. I remember some particular friends who had just dropped by, as they talked to me I told them I couldn't see properly. They immediately stopped the conversation and walked away. This really hurt me; I will never know what was going through their heads at that time, maybe they didn't know what to say. But they didn't have to treat me so differently.

Yvonne dropped me home later and I found my uncle and Mum a bit worried since we were slightly late. I went straight to bed only to wake up some time in the night to eat. That routine had been going on for a while. I would always feel very hungry at night, even after I had had my dinner, hence would wake up to eat fruit, salad, bread and juice. I was told that it was one of the after effects of the surgery and also I needed to raise my blood level. So Mum always made sure she left the food where I could easily find it in the dark whenever the cravings struck. Eating at such wee hours of the night made me to increase my weight. I had mastered the kitchen and I could feel my way round the room without knocking over utensils and clattering them everywhere.

Over the next few days we visited several people's homes. Some invited us for dinner, others lunch. In almost all homes, we were treated with great hospitality and as honoured guests. A prayer was said before we left each home. Words cannot express the gratitude Mum and I felt towards the selfless nature of this community living in the diaspora. They counted not the costs they incurred, but willingly opened their homes to let us in to dine and share a good laugh with them. Some of the people included Paul Makoko and his family, who had been one of the founders of the community's spirit of togetherness. Mama Kokome, an elderly lady whose soft-spoken and very charming nature made us enjoy her company. Makrina, Lindiwe's Mum, was a wonderful and hardworking person who enticed us with her scrumptious cuisine and friendly personality. Jamal, a dedicated and dependable person with his wife Kursa and their lovely children Shamsa, 8, and Jamu, 4, rejuvenated my spirits by making me get in touch with my childhood as they would make me play with their toys and watch their Disney animations. I would get lost in their fantasy worlds, laugh and play with them as though I was their age. As we played, I couldn't help pick up Jamu and swing him around; his sweet laughter was infectious as he enjoyed our little play. Mum would tell me to put him down since I was not allowed to lift anything heavier than a gallon of milk; he was way over that limit, but I couldn't resist.

There was Yusta, Paul's niece, a very talkative, cheerful and hardworking person who would drop by almost every evening after work since she lived close by. She treated me like her younger sister, we would watch many movies together and have a laugh during hilarious scenes or be very sad at the end of a moving story. Casmille, a calm, entertaining, dependable and dedicated person, also invited us to his home and went out of his way to entertain us for meals. His family was back in Tanzania and he lived with Billy, his client. Billy always had never ending stories and would make me laugh the entire time I spent with him. However when it came to duties and chores, he was very hardworking and a clean freak.

There were two ladies both named Eliza. One lived by herself in a nice apartment; she was a nurse. Her hearty laughter was catching, and there was no way one could sit with her for even a minute without bursting into laughter. The other was Eliza

Franko. She lived with her husband, Mr. Franko, an even toned man, who smiled a lot and made short but funny statements, and their daughter, Mary. Eliza was a fashionable middle-aged lady whose shrill voice was distinct as soon as she opened her mouth to speak. I always singled out her voice in a group of people.

There were other people as well: Mapenzi and his wife, Mama Bhoke, Lucas and his wife, Mama Lisa, Bupe, Magdalena, Elias, Obed, Hashim, Saburi and his wife, Edna, Siraji, a young man, who would lend us his movies to keep me and Mum occupied at home. He was also a kind and dedicated person with subtle humour. There was also Pauline, a Kenyan lady who had just received a delicate operation. The positivity emanating from her speech was inspiring as she praised God for having spared her life. There were many more people who invited us or visited likewise. It was always great company to be with them. Not only did they offer their company and food, but also get well soon gifts and little tokens. Others even offered to do our grocery shopping and would adamantly refuse whenever Mum or my uncle wanted to reimburse them.

The youngsters were not left out either. Mapenzi's children, Bhoke, Grace, Wankyo and Janet, together with Yvonne and Daniel came one evening and we ordered pizza and watched a couple of movies. We also took a couple of photos that Mum later used to point out who the different individuals were. I had an indistinct idea of how they looked, so I was more confident when talking to them whenever I saw them again.

While watching the movies, my eyes would really squint in order to see the images on the screen. I also sat very close to the TV so that I could at least watch the movies properly, but it was difficult and uncomfortable. Despairingly, I would rely on Mum's description of actors.

Apart from watching movies, we would go shopping or sight-seeing. In the malls, Mum held my hand so I wouldn't collide with people. She did most of the selecting since all I could see were colours; rarely would I see the designs. Uncle Peter pointed out some sites such as ancient churches, city hall and elderly citizens' homes, schools, malls, car dealers and fast food restaurants as we drove by. Sometimes I would see them, other times I wouldn't no matter how much I tried, and they would seem like red brick warehouses or just ordinary buildings. One day he took us to a ski resort, just to have a look. From where we stood all I could see was a mountain of snow and the evergreen conifers huddled together in some areas. I couldn't see the people. However I could hear cheers and screams emerging from somewhere up in the mountains. My uncle and Mum could see the skiers, and told me that people were cheering on their teammates as they swiftly skied down the mountain. Uncle Peter and I had a snowball fight as Mum looked on, warning me to be careful not to fall in the snow since my incisions were still tender.

In the evenings I would at times ask Mum to read my emails for me. Gradually, I realized I could see some letters and even words. In order to read something, a sign, title or address, I would tilt my head narrowly sideways and upwards then slowly spell out the words. I was only able to read large fonts for the small ones still appeared closely knit together. Every morning I would wake up expecting to see more than the previous day, and sometimes I was right, other times there was no significant change. Either way, it was not deteriorating so I was grateful. Time went by, sometimes fast, sometimes slowly.

The days for our trip back to Tanzania drew closer. Aunt Anna had insisted that she wanted to see me before I went back home. She wanted to be sure that my health had improved as well as my vision. Hence on Friday 7th March at around 4pm we embarked on the long drive to Maryland. It was a rainy night, so my uncle had to slow down once in a while when the road got too slippery. We arrived around midnight, absolutely exhausted. She was so happy to see us. I was glad to see her. I could see the thin lines of wrinkles that showed her advancement in age; her tired eyes indicated she had had a long day but her sweet smile and hearty laughter resounded in the room. We had a late supper as my aunt narrated her childhood experiences with her cousin, my uncle chipping in once in a while, and about my grandparents, most of whom had passed away. It was a great trip down memory lane. It was a great night. Soon I retired to bed earlier than everyone else. As I walked up the stairs, I noticed a photo of a young, chubby boy. I moved closer and studied the picture. I noticed the fair skinned boy with bright round eyes. My aunt told me it was Baraka, her grandson. I also noticed the African art-along the stairs and the sitting room; big beautifully decorated pots, gourds and skillfully handmade carvings. Aunt Anna appreciates African art that explains the décor in her house. I couldn't see the minute details but at least I could see enough to avoid knocking them over. I even noticed my aunt's large room, with it's extensive walk-in closet.

I woke up the next morning to find the smell of my aunt frying some eggs. It was cold and rainy that Saturday morning. The four of us had a slow, lazy breakfast. As we ate, we discussed the plans for the day. By the time we were done, the rain had reduced to a drizzle and some rays of sun peeped through the grey clouds. We first headed to the Seventh Day Adventist (SDA) General Conference in Washington, DC. This is the headquarters of the SDA church worldwide. I squinted to read the white banner with blue writing at the entrance and was able to do so with slight difficulty. After we had walked round the premises, we headed out to meet Violet, who had also requested to see me before my return home. We spent just a few minutes together and this time I was glad I could see her face slightly more than the last time. She was just as Mum had described her: fair-skinned with a distinct beauty gap between her front teeth. We left her and then headed to Grand Central for a tour round DC. As we approached it, my uncle pointed out the House of Congress from a distance. I tried to see it, but it took me a while before the dome-shaped building came into view.

At the station, we parted with Aunt Anna because after our tour we had to drive to New Jersey to visit some of my uncle's friends. As she bade us farewell, I could see her moist eyes even though she tried to hide them behind her tinted glasses. I really wanted to stay one extra day with her, but we had a number of places and people to visit before our approaching return to Tanzania.

By the time we started the tour it was late in the afternoon. Although the sun was shining, we held our jackets tighter due to the cold, blustery weather. The tour was disappointing since no sooner had we started, than it gradually grew dark outside due to the early sunset during the winter season. This automatically made the little vision I had hopeless as I could only see the dim lights that had come on in the sites as the tour guide pointed them out. Some of the sites included the House of Congress, the White House, The Lincoln Memorial, the US Capital Building and the World War 2 Memorial. Out of all these, I was only able to see the Congress building and the War memorial, since they stand out as one goes round the city. Had my eyes been okay, I would surely have enjoyed the serene night tour.

Finally the tour came to an end and we got into the car and drove off to New Jersey. After a long drive, we arrived at the house of Aunt Virginia's nephew, Martin. The house was in pitch darkness since the strong wind had caused the transformer to break down, thus discontinuing electricity supply in the entire neighbourhood. Our hosts, of whom I did not even have an inkling how they looked despite the candles and torches they had lit, were very warm and chatty people. It was unfortunate that I left their house without knowing how they looked. I was only able to see them later from the photos that Mum had taken.

The next day we headed to New York for a day tour. It was much better than the previous one since we went during midday and the sun shone beautifully as we sat on the open tour bus feeling the slight cold chill that challenged the sun. I saw the Empire State Building, since it stood out due to its unique architectural design. Apart from it, I only vaguely saw the other attractions. I just listened to the entertaining tour guide as he pointed out the different sites. We passed through crowded streets with the famous yellow taxis; typical New York, just like in the movies. We passed the fashion boulevards, Wall Street's high-rise banks, and famous movie locations like Central Park, Brooklyn Bridge, Manhattan and also Ground Zero where the Twin towers had once stood.

Honestly, I felt slightly depressed, being in one of the world's most famous cities but not being able to fully take in the scenery. However, I was still grateful that at least I had some vision and could distinguish between people and objects.

Apart from the Empire State, I was only eager to see the Statue of Liberty. As we approached it, I tried to behold its beauty towering above us as we circled round it with the ferry. It was quite a sight to behold, I was glad I had finally set my feeble eyes on that amazing beauty. By the time the tour was over, it was approaching late afternoon, so we briskly walked to the car for our onward journey back to Massachusetts. We arrived there at around 11pm, completely exhausted but satisfied with the fulfilling weekend.

On Wednesday, 12th March, I had an appointment with Dr. Julie to check on the healing progress of the incisions. A few days before, I had noticed that one incision hadn't healed as well as the other two. She saw it and prescribed an antibiotic cream and urged me to keep it covered in order to prevent infections. Aside from that, she was pleased with my general progress and wished me a safe trip back home. She scheduled an appointment at the beginning of June. Little did we know we would see each other sooner than the early blooms of the spring.

Once she had authorised our trip, I was overjoyed since the following week, on the 20th of March, we were heading back to Tanzania. I couldn't wait to see Dad, my relatives and friends. I couldn't wait to behold the breathtaking sunrise and golden sunset in my hometown or the majestic full moon illuminating with all its glory. Oh, how I had missed all these things.

Unfortunately, as the week progressed, it became clear that the incision was not getting better. In fact it got worse every day. It was itchy, hence making me gently scratch around it. Mum told me not to, but secretly I did since it made it feel better for a while. But that would only invigorate the intensity of the itch. When Mum had a look at it, she noticed the incision was inflamed. This made her more concerned. I was applying the cream as directed, but it didn't seem to reduce the inflammation or the itch. One night, the incision began to ooze a certain fluid, and this made me panic. Fortunately, I had an appointment with a Primary Care Physician, Dr. Annette that Monday 17th March. As she tested my vision, I told her how excited I was about going back to Tanzania but was concerned about the incision. She then had a look at it and from her tone I could tell she was deeply concerned. She excused herself to go and get her superior. As we sat with Mum waiting for her to return, I quickly dismissed the possibility that we would have to cancel our trip. I was almost certain they would prescribe me something I could use back home. Dr Annette returned with her superior as promised. He seemed equally concerned when he saw the infected incision. He called Dr. Julie, who couldn't make it that evening but requested to see me the very next day. Before we left, he swabbed a sample of the fluid to send to the laboratory for further tests. Deep inside I was beginning to doubt the underestimation I had made about the persistent infection. The doctors seemed concerned; clearly there was something I was not seeing which had nothing to do with my vision. I felt another itch, as though it was gloating over me.

The next morning we began packing. Two more days, and we couldn't wait. This time round I was slightly more helpful during the packing, and it was a relief. Every little thing I did that I couldn't do before was an indication of an improvement. We left everything lying around so that we could finish packing up once we had got back from the hospital. As we sat in the waiting room waiting to be called upon, I looked around the room. I noticed the lounge chairs, some occupied, others not. I saw the big potted plant next to one of the pillars, the water dispenser next to me, the receptionist's desk cluttered with brochures and flyers. I noticed things I hadn't seen before whenever I went for my appointments. It was great to witness these new things.

We were called in shortly afterwards by the nurse and told to wait for Dr. Julie. She came in soon and examined the incision. That is when I noticed how tall she was, her warm smile, her half-clipped or tied black hair which I realized months later in a photograph was actually auburn. Clearly I was still having difficulty with colour details, such as the white lab coat she wore. It was refreshing to finally have a glimpse of the person who had operated on me. She momentarily left the room to get the lab results.

She came back shortly after and said,

"I'm sorry Margareth, but it looks like you won't be travelling to Africa as soon as you had hoped."

"What do you mean doctor?" I asked, clearly alarmed.

"According to the test results, your incision tested positive for an infection. So we have to perform further surgery before the infection reaches your spinal cord."

"How could it happen? Does that usually happen?" I inquired, completely caught off guard.

"Yes; since our bodies have countless bacteria in them, some helpful while others are harmful, we are prone to infections. The foreign hardware we inserted in your body makes it an easy target for the harmful bacteria, hence the infection," she explained.

"Is there no other way to deal with the infection apart from surgery? Antibiotics maybe?" I quizzed, hoping to hear the latter was an option.

"I'm afraid not in your case. We don't know how far the infection has spread and wouldn't want to take any chances," she asserted firmly.

"So, when am I scheduled for the surgery?" I asked in surrender.

"Tomorrow. You are already on the waiting list for tomorrow morning. There is not a single moment to spare."

"Unbelievable! I never would have thought this evening I would be sleeping in UMASS and waking up to surgery tomorrow. And to think we had already started packing!" I quipped.

"I'm sorry, but I am actually glad the problem has revealed itself now before you travel. It would have slowly spread and before it was detected it would have been too serious to treat."

"You are right. Thank God it will be solved soon." I smiled weakly.

"The nurses will come and pick you up shortly to take you to your room for admission." She mentioned.

Uncle Peter and Mum, who had been silent this whole time, were as shocked as I was. They did not know what to do or say. Plans had drastically changed. After a moment to let the news sink in, my uncle said,

"It's true, it would have been worse if she had travelled back home."

Dr. Julie then added, "Infact, had the infection spread to the spinal cord, it would have led to a serious case of meningitis."

"Praise be to God for preventing such a catastrophe and thanks to you doctor, for detecting it," Mum exclaimed.

The doctor went on to say, "Tomorrow's surgery is not a major one. We will only remove the infected shunt, replace it with a catheter for about a week. The catheter is a tube with a bag where the excess fluid which flowed through the shunt, will drain in. And for that one week, we will have to intravenously disinfect you with antibiotics so as to kill off any bacteria before placing a new shunt."

"How long will the procedure take?" I asked.

"Approximately half an hour to an hour..." she replied.

"So I guess no eating after midnight?" I said.

"Yes, you already know the drill. Any more questions?" she asked.

I turned and looked at Mum and my uncle sitting beside me. They seemed to be sighing deep inside. I just shook my head and looked down at my hand for distraction. My uncle asked if he could get a letter from her confirming the impromptu surgery so as to take it to the ticket office in order to change our flight. She told him she would write one up as soon as she got back to her office. Then she hurriedly left the room.

As soon as she had left, Mum and I burst out laughing at the way we had left the room in a mess, thinking we would finish packing after the appointment. We mused at the fact that we were not going to be going to Tanzania for another month or so. All our hopes and plans had come crashing down. On one hand I was disappointed for not travelling; however on the other hand I was grateful that the problem had been identified in advance.

The nurse came and injected the IV into my arm, I was back to the hospital drill. As she wheeled me off to the fourth floor she asked me if I had been admitted there before. I replied affirmatively.

Then she said,

"Yeah, I remember you. You couldn't see, right? It was so sad seeing you like that."

"Yes, I couldn't see then but now my vision has improved slightly. I can even see you're wearing a blue tunic." I replied.

"That's great dear. Though I'm sorry you've had to come back."

"Yeah, it's quite unfortunate, but maybe I'm back because last time I didn't get to see all the wonderful people who were attending to me," I said, smiling

"Oh dear, that's sweet of you to say" she said with obvious appreciation.

As I approached the room, I could vaguely see the corridors and different rooms. I could distinguish the nurses from the visitors. I could see some empty wheelchairs and laundry trolleys at the end of the corridor. I was seeing the hospital from a whole new perspective - it wasn't dark anymore. I wasn't passing blindly through the corridors. I was noticing things, something I couldn't do before. I was happy. When I got into the room there was another patient. A large flowery curtain was drawn up to separate us. Uncle Peter stayed for a while before heading out to get us some food.

Mum then phoned Aunt Virginia to inform her of my re-admission. She was so shocked since she had been with me the day before when we had seen Dr. Annette. Mum also informed Dad that he wouldn't be seeing us as soon as we had hoped. I could hear his distressing tone as he spoke to us. He had been eagerly waiting to see us and now plans had unexpectedly changed. I was sure he was miserable for not being near me at that time.

After my uncle came back, we ate and talked for a while before they left for the night. I lay on my back watching TV. At least this time I could see some of the images on the screen, unlike the last time when I even had a problem locating the TV itself. I couldn't sleep so I kept asking the nurse for some snacks before midnight; my favourite, orange sherbet.

I had noticed my fellow roommate had a caretaker so I asked the latter what she was suffering from. She told me the patient had a mental condition, but was hospitalized for pneumonia. No wonder she is wheezing and also keeps asking for a drink, I thought. As we continued talking I found out that the caretaker was a Kenyan, this made us chat for a long time. I carefully got out of bed and went over to her side of the room. I looked down at the patient lying on her back smiling up at me. She reached for my hand in greeting and I gently clasped it. We talked for a while until the nurse came to check my vitals. I slept shortly after.

The next morning, Wednesday, 19th March, I woke up and anxiously waited for Mum to show up. I was allowed to take breakfast since my surgery wasn't at that time until later in the afternoon. The anesthetist had come for his procedural preparation and had told me the anesthesia they would use wouldn't knock me out completely; it would only make me numb to the pain. Mum finally came, I told her about the Kenyan lady I had conversed with the previous night, who by that time had left and been replaced with another. Mum called Dad and we talked and he prayed for the surgery ahead.

Shortly after, I was wheeled off to the preparation area where the anesthetists were waiting together with a nurse. Mum did not come with me this time. After the preparation procedures it was time to head out to the theatre. This time I did not black out immediately like the first time; I could faintly see people, equipment, double doors, and elevators, as we crisscrossed the corridors.

I was awake up to the time I entered the theatre. I could dimly see the big lights above me and some of the scrubs, then I don't recall what happened next. Next thing I remember waking up as though from a deep sleep and from a distance hearing people talking. I tried opening my eyes but they were too heavy and only opened as slits. From a distance I thought I heard someone say, "Don't worry Margareth, we're almost done..." It seemed to me like a dream.

I then closed my eyes, but could feel a couple of hands on my body and felt a cool liquid splash on my side. My feeble body couldn't move; it was as though it had been barricaded on both sides. Unable to fully open my eyes and comprehend my whereabouts, I slowly fell back into an unconscious state.

I then woke up and strained to call out for help, my throat hurt a bit. A nurse rushed and calmed me down. After some time, she took me back to my room. Mum was there waiting together with Geliga. They prayed as soon as the nurse had left the room. I was given food and then slept. When I woke up, I demanded to go to the bathroom, but I was given a bedpan to use until I was strong enough to walk. I could feel the catheter from the spine then hanging on my bedside. I could feel the fresh bandages where the incisions were.

Dr. Julie came later to see how I was holding up.

"How are you feeling, Margareth?" she asked silently.

"Tire with a slight headache," I replied with my voice frail.

"That is because the catheter has not been allowed to drain the fluid into the bag. I will have a nurse open the bag every two hours so as to release the accumulated fluid into the bag," she said reassuringly.

"What happens when the bag fills up?" I asked curiously.

"A neurologist will come and replace it with a new bag. They are the only people allowed to handle the bag since the fluid is delicate and any minor mishandling may affect the liquid that is still in the catheter. Any leakage may also increase the severity of the headaches so the nurses have to ensure the catheter is securely closed."

She left shortly after that, promising to check up on me over the next few days. That same day, I was scheduled to have an appointment with the hematologist to check on the progress of my blood level. Since I was admitted and couldn't go to see him, he took blood samples and sent them to the laboratory.

On Thursday 20th March, we sat with Mum in the room, thinking of how we would have been flying home that day. We just laughed at the irony of the whole situation. Friday 21 March, I got several visitors in the evening. Yvonne and Lindiwe came with Uncle Peter. We talked about how I was doing and they told me about how their week had been. We laughed and had a good time, they cheered me up. Jamal also came with his entire family. He also came with Steven, Evarist's friend who had come for medical reasons as well. Jamu didn't dare to look at me. He cried when he saw me lying on the bed with the catheter hanging from my side. They left shortly after Mum, Uncle Peter, Yvonne and Lindiwe stayed on for a while and helped me to eat. We talked some more things before they left. I felt lonely that night after they had left as I had wanted them to stay longer.

I had trouble sleeping, for I woke up every time the nurses came to drain the catheter, which was after every two hours. I was also uncomfortable since I could only lie on my back and not on either of my sides. I asked for the time whenever the nurses came to drain the catheter. Time dragged on through the night. I dreamt of Mum sitting beside me only to wake up, enveloped in darkness and surrounded with beeping machines and a distant scuffling of people in the corridor. From some room a man shouted for a nurse; he needed to use the bathroom. Another lady screamed at how incompetent the nurses were and how she wanted to leave the hospital that very night. The groaning and whining contributed even more to a restless night.

Eventually after the unpleasant night, I fell asleep in the morning. I slept so soundly only to wake up at the sweet aroma of my breakfast and find Mum sitting beside me reading her Bible. She served me the breakfast and watched me eat as I grumbled about my night. The day wore on with occasional visitors from time to time, but most of the time it was just me and Mum.

Later, Uncle Peter came as soon as he was back from church. Yusta also came to visit and brought me a get well soon, helium balloon which she tied to the top of my bed. She didn't stay for long but I was glad she had come. The rest of the day went by slowly, the sun was shining outside but I didn't have the pleasure of enjoying it.

Sunday, 23rd March, before Mum arrived, Dr. Julie came and told me that they had postponed the surgery from the next day to Wednesday, 24th March. She said they needed to be sure that the infection had completely been eradicated before inserting the new shunt. She was glad that I was responding well to the antibiotics. I then told her of an incident that had happened when I began using the antibiotics intravenously.

"My body started feeling itchy and hot. It felt swollen and gave me a lot of discomfort. So I had to call the nurse," I narrated.

"I was informed. It happened because the medicine was flowing into your system at a fast rate, hence causing the reaction. But you are alright now, since we gave you the tablets instead?" she inquired.

"Yes, I'm not having any problem with them. I was scared when it happened since I thought it was an allergic reaction," I said.

"We are glad it wasn't," she said.

When Mum came later that day, I told her what the doctor had said regarding my surgery. Then she told me that Elias would be coming with a certain Pr. Dan who was going to give me a healing anointing. They came and after all formal introductions had taken place, Pr. Dan prayed. He then read from the scriptures and explained that the healing anointing wasn't offered often and that it wasn't an assurance of being healed immediately, it was just a special anointing. When it came to the anointing itself, he applied some oil on my forehead and then he and Elias placed their hands on my head and prayed. After the prayers they did not stay much longer. I tried to catch a glimpse of the two visitors, but wasn't so successful. All I could tell was that Elias, whom I had met before and who was Mapenzi's brother, was a middle-aged man with a calm way of speaking. Pr. Dan was a Caucasian man in his late fifties or early sixties who spoke with a firm, quivery voice. Mum then told me how special I was since I had received the anointing. The rest of the day wore on. Now that the surgery had been postponed it meant I had a longer stay at the hospital. I was already tired of being there. I called my brothers and told them of my forthcoming surgery, and they pitied me.

The next two days went by without anything significant happening. Dr. Julie showed up to explain how the procedure was going to take place. It was just like the first time, only this time it would go through my right side. Wednesday 26th March, I went in for my third surgery in two months. I prayed that this would be my last one. Mum came in the morning before I was wheeled off and let me talk to Dad before going to the theatre. And just like the first surgery, I blacked out before heading to the theatre and woke up in the recovery room some hours later.

I was lying flat on my back with no pillow to support my head. I tried to get up but was too weak to do so. Then a nurse came and as he wheeled me off to my room, he asked what I had gone into surgery for. I feebly explained to him. He was sympathetic as he went on to say,

"It's such a pity for a young girl like you to go through all this."

When we got into the room he saw the radio which my uncle had brought for me. He asked the kind of music I listened to on the radio.

"Country music," I proudly told him.

"Country! Are you serious?" he exclaimed, obviously amused at my statement, "You're the first young person I've met who listens to country. It's for old people like us."

"I get that reaction every time I say that. But I like the music because most of the time it tells a story and it is sensual," I responded.

"You've made my day," he said as he finally positioned my bed in its rightful place.

He then told my uncle that I was a very interesting person. He wished me a quick recovery and then left. Mum was just happy to see that I had come back safe. The nurse in charge later came and told me that I was required to lie flat on my back for 24 hours.

"What? 24 hours? But I'm already tired lying on my back," I complained.

"I'm sorry but those are the doctor's instructions dear. It is so that the pressure in your body balances."

"Not even a thin pillow to slightly elevate my head?" I moaned.

"I'm afraid not. Don't worry, it will be over before you know it," she enthused.

I whimpered, but nothing could be done. As usual, I was hungry so Mum fed me the mashed potatoes and gravy. It was an incredibly difficult task to eat while lying flat on the back. I kept thinking that the food would pass though my nose at some point. I even felt like I was out of breath as I ate since my stomach felt bloated and was panting at the end of the heavy meal. After the prolonged lunch, I slept, not because I was sleepy but because I wanted time to fly by. This was going to be the most uncomfortable 24 hours of my life. I could only turn my head from side to side, even when people came to greet me. The rest of the day just went by slowly, and I wasn't able to sleep. Soon it was time for Mum and Uncle Peter to leave. I was once again alone.

I tried sleeping despite the discomfort. I kept counting down the hours every time a nurse told me the time. When I needed to use the bathroom, the nurse would slowly turn me to my left side then put in a bedpan. It was utterly uncomfortable and slightly humiliating. I couldn't wait for the hours to be over. The position was so uncomfortable, I hated the idea of ever lying on my back again. Well, of course I forgot that shortly after the 24 hours were up.

Finally morning came, just a few hours left before the torture was over and I could elevate myself. There was no way I was going to drink tea in that position so I sipped some juice using a straw and waited for 10am to have a proper breakfast. As soon as the time was up, I elevated my bed and then turned to my side - what a relief! I was more energetic and kept Mum entertained with my ever-lasting stories.

Uncle Peter had a meeting on Friday, so he had to catch a flight to Texas that evening. Dr. Julie advised me to lie in an elevated position once I got home. She then told me I would be cleared by the physiotherapist and then I could be discharged. The physiotherapist came that Friday evening and discharged me after carrying out a couple of exercises. She made me walk up and down a flight of stairs in order to check on my stability, then advised me to have similar walks once I got back home.

Later, Jamal came to pick us up from the hospital with his daughter, Shamsa. He wheeled me off to his car after saying bye to the hospital staff that I had grown fond of. As soon as I stood up from the wheelchair to get into the car, I felt my head spin fast and almost lost balance before Mum quickly grabbed me. Jamal then adjusted the front seat and straightened it down so that I could lie down during the drive since my head would spin if I sat up straight. I lay in that position for the entire half hour drive in the drizzly night. When we got home, Jamal helped us offload our things as Mum helped me inside. Yvonne was there and had prepared dinner. We ate, then I went off to bed, glad to be home but sick of the spinning headache. Nevertheless, the rain outside beckoned me to sleep.

In the morning, Mum helped me to get ready, then I had my breakfast and went back to sleep. I wanted to keep her company since we were just the two of us, but she dismissed me saying that I needed to rest. I woke up just in time for lunch and found out that we had visitors. Geliga had come with his daughter, Rachel whom I hadn't met before and his in-law, Obed, a very talkative individual. Mum had prepared some ugali, a typical African dish, and fried fish, which I hurriedly ate. Then I went to lie down in my room for I couldn't sit up for long without having a headache. Rachel followed me to the room to keep me company. I couldn't see her face properly, but I noticed her slender figure and height slightly taller than me. She told me that she was at home for spring break and that she was studying dentistry in Maryland. She then asked me about myself, and I told her about my aspiration to study law and become a judge. We then had a debate about job opportunities for women in Africa. She hadn't been to Tanzania in a while, so she thought women were still being discriminated in the job market. I told her of how the government was prioritizing women in many different sectors.

The discussion was interrupted when more guests arrived. Amina, Paul's daughter, came. Her distinct, high-pitched voice made her stand out. I couldn't see her face, but could see her sweet smile. She and Rachel got talking, catching up on things as they had not seen each other for a while. As they talked, Rehema came with her uncle and aunt. We talked with Rehema as Amina and Rachel headed out to visit Yusta. I had not seen her in a while so it was great catching up on life. I noticed her warm smile, chocolate-skinned face contrary to the fair one I had in mind and her soft voice made her an easy person to talk with. We talked for a while before she left.

Bored of being in the room for the whole day, I dragged my feet to the sitting room to join Mum and Edna, who were watching a movie. The next few hours just flew by amidst laughter and criticisms of certain characters. Edna then left as Mum and I went on watching the movie before we slept.

My uncle came back that Sunday at around midnight. In the following days people came to see how I was getting on. This time round I followed instructions. I never lifted any heavy objects; including kids, no matter how irresistible they were, or ran around the house. I was not going back to the hospital for letting my incisions not heal properly. When I became strong enough, Mum would take me for walks around the apartment. We would set a different target in terms of distance to cover. The early spring leaves and flowers had bloomed, the place turned green almost overnight. The snow had thawed and was replaced with fresh green lawns. I began to notice my surroundings-the red brick block of flats with slightly tinted glass doors, spread out in different complexes, the different cars that were parked outside, the fire hydrant, the once-bare trees now with new leaves, the factory further down from the apartment, the slope that always indicated we needed to take a right to reach home. It was overwhelming being able to see all these things. Whenever it rained, our walks were confined to the set of stairs from the ground floor to the topmost floors. These moments brought me and Mum closer. We laughed together; she held my hand when I couldn't go up a certain flight of stairs. I held hers when she stopped in the middle and gasped for air since she has a weak chest.

When I was strong enough to be on my feet for long, we went shopping. We would spend long hours at the mall with Mum, sometimes buying other times just window shopping. When I got tired Mum would notice my growing disinterest in shopping. After observing so many different items, my eyes would begin to fail me and I would strain to see. Mum then told me my eyes had turned red so we stopped shopping and waited for my uncle to come and pick us up. When we got home, I would straightaway go to bed.

Our daily routines went on for days. Days went by till it was time to see Dr. Julie so that she could allow me to travel, depending on my progress. I went with Mum and Aunt Virginia. She was happy with my general health and commented at how beautifully the incisions had healed. She granted my trip and scheduled an appointment for early June. I was so happy and thanked her immensely. Mum and Aunt Virginia also expressed their deepest gratitude. Dr. Julie then said,

"I have to be honest with you. The shunt we had placed at first was computer programmed and the latest technology we have. It requires one to have regular check-ups and also needs to be closely monitored. So, when you told me you were going back to Africa I was a bit worried in case something happened to it. You might not have received the immediate attention it requires. For example, if you went very near an object with a strong magnetic field, the shunt would automatically shut down," she confessed.

"What about the one you have put in now?" I asked, clearly taken aback by that confession.

"Well that one is mechanical. That is why your headaches didn't disappear as fast as when you had the other one. Honestly, when you came with that infected incision, I knew it was a blessing in disguise. That is when we decided to change to the one that would be more convenient," she explained.

We were all silent for a moment before Aunt Virginia exclaimed, "Praise God!"

I just sat there whispering a prayer of thanksgiving to God. Back in March when the doctor had told us we wouldn't be travelling, we were disappointed, we complained and grumbled. Little did we know that it was a way of God stalling our journey in order for me to receive the treatment required-serendipity maybe? I was thankful to Dr. Julie again. She wished us a safe trip back home.

After leaving the hospital that day, I really reflected on how blessed I was. God still had a plan for me. I thanked Him for giving my parents the means to provide for my hospitalization and the unexpected trip. We began preparing to travel back to Tanzania. We had been away from home for almost three months. I couldn't wait to go back. Mum's friend had told her how Dad had lost weight and just looked sad and depressed. I couldn't wait to go and embrace him dearly.

On 19th April, there was a youth day at the village church and later lunch at Paul's house. It was great hanging out with everyone. They had all been really accommodating to Mum and me for the whole time we had been there. They had accepted us as part of their society. We will forever be grateful. It was a bit emotional bidding farewell to all these people who had dedicated their time and resources to us. I went to Leominster unable to see at all, but left being able to identify most of their faces.

Part Four

Monday, 21st April, the day I had been waiting for a very long time. I was really looking forward to go back home to Tanzania. So many people were longing to see me back there. Part of me had grown to love this Massachusetts community, but east-west home is best. It was sad to leave Uncle Peter. He had really gotten used to having us around. He didn't feel so bad for he knew we would be back in June. We flew from Logan International Airport in Boston to Amsterdam and finally to Julius Nyerere International Airport in Dar-es-Salaam. As we approached the city, Mum asked me to look out of the window. I could see the distant, sparsely-distributed lights. I could see them!

As we waited for our luggage I looked at the conveyor belt full of luggage, the airport trolleys, fellow passengers who thronged around to get their luggage, airport security going about their business. I could vaguely see all these activities. My relatives who were waiting for us were: Uncle Andrew, his wife, and Chaya. They embraced us warmly. Uncle Andrew wanted to test my vision so he asked me if I could see the fingers he held up. I tilted my face and looked at him sideways and said,

"It's night so my eyes are not particularly powerful. But I can see you are wearing a Chelsea jersey. Are you a fan?"

He burst out laughing and said,

"I can see you as well. And yes, I'm a fan and we are playing tonight."

We continued laughing as they helped us to the car with our luggage. To Mum's surprise, Ken came and embraced her. She was so shocked to see him there because they had talked over the phone on the morning we left the USA while he was in Dubai. I then told her how I had planned with Ken for him to come from Dubai to meet us. Ken was wearing a safari hat so he looked like a tourist. They were all happy to see that I could at least recognize them. I saw their kind faces and warm smiles. We had a deliciously long dinner at Uncle Andrew's house, as Mum narrated our entire experience while in USA. We then retired off to bed at a hotel which Ken had booked for us. It was the same hotel at which we had had lunch on the afternoon he'd left for Dubai back in January.

Dad hadn't come to meet us at the airport since he had travelled to China on a business trip. He was, however, getting back on that Thursday and I couldn't wait to see him. Every time I said that word I smiled at how far I had come in four months.

Since we had arrived on Tuesday, we had the whole of Wednesday to get over the jetlag as we waited for Dad to arrive the next day. We spent the whole day at the hotel entertaining visits from some family friends and relatives. I was glad I could see them, and they were happy I had come back better than I had left. They praised God. Chaya was one of the people who were so surprised to see my improvement because he had been there from the day I lost my sight. Seeing me walking unaided, despite missing one or two steps as I walked down the stairs and even texting on my own was nothing short of a miracle. Ken didn't say much as he was amazed beyond words. It was really thoughtful of him to come to see us after returning from my hospitalization. I called and texted my friends informing them of my return. They had endless questions about how I was, if my sight had fully recovered, what were the doctors saying. I just laughed and briefly explained that I was fine and was taking each day as it came.

Thursday, 24th April, we made sure we were at the airport before Dad arrived from his trip. Mum pointed him out as he collected his luggage. I couldn't see him since the doors had a reflecting surface. However, as soon as he walked out through the exit, I ran over and embraced him. I couldn't help but shed a tear. I could see my father again. I touched his face as though I couldn't believe he was standing right in front of me. I noticed he had lost some weight and had a few more tired lines that showed a man who had been in pain. It was evident that he had been having a really rough time during the past couple of months. I didn't want to let go of him. He had come with Freddy, Chaya's older brother. He was also really happy to see me, even though he hadn't seen me during my lowest moments.

We went back to the hotel and Mum had to narrate the whole experience to them. Before she began, Dad offered a prayer of thanksgiving to God. He thanked Him for my health, the progressing recovery of my sight, Mum's health, the safe journey and finally the happy reunion. We spent the whole day catching up and just enjoying that wonderful moment. Dad also handed me a bunch of letters my friends who were also my juniors back in school had written. I struggled to read them but I gave up and promised to read them as soon as I could read properly.

Friday, 25th April, Uncle Mashauri and his wife came to see us. They were happy to see me better than I had been at Hope Hospital. Later we went to see Dr. Bwana and his family. I was very happy to see them. Their warm hearts were equally glad. He then told me, "Don't forget your books are still waiting for you." We all burst out laughing. Tina was not there though; she had gone back to school. This time I was also able to see that their house was white and not pink like the last time. We didn't stay for long because we had a flight to catch that evening, onward to Mwanza where Lucky was eagerly waiting for us. We also bid Ken farewell since he was returning to Dubai the following day.

At the airport, our flight got delayed for over two hours. This was very frustrating for I couldn't wait to see Lucky. When we finally made our flight and arrived in Mwanza, I gazed around at the airport I had left months earlier, before I lost my sight. I was overjoyed to see Lucky. We had a lot of catching up to do. I had really missed him, and seeing his gentle face and big dark brown eyes reminded me of how much I had missed him. I wasn't afraid to look closely at his face since he is among the family members. As usual he made fun with the fact that one of my eyes was still looking sideways. Secretly, I knew he was happy that I had made it through the worst.

Saturday, 26th April, was a very emotional day. We drove home, Musoma, from Mwanza. During the entire journey, I looked out of the window at the people on the road, the little shops, the warehouses, the vast grasslands, distant hills and the majestic

Lake Victoria. I was home, I had made it back. As we got into the compound, I could hear singing and jubilation. I could see so many people. My parents got out of the car first and everyone waited anxiously for me to make my grand exit. As I emerged out of the car, I saw my grandmothers, aunts, uncles, cousins, neighbours, pastors, church members and other well-wishers. I broke down into tears as I tried to hug everyone at once. Some cried with me, but Mum told them not to for God had already brought me through the worst and they should all just be thankful.

I was escorted to my room by my grandmothers and aunts. As I sat on the bed and continued crying for the next few minutes, I could not even utter a word. I was overcome with deep emotion. Through my teary eyes, I looked around the room over and over again at the eager faces of my loved ones. I finally composed myself after my grandmothers held my hands and rubbed my back as they told me to stop crying. Through sniffles I just told them,

"I'm not crying because I am sad but because I am thinking I would never have seen all of you again."

Some of them stifled mumbled cries. I just thanked God that I was at home and seeing all these people was just a miracle. Every time I think about this day, I still get slightly emotional. We were later called to the sitting room for they had organized a thanksgiving service. Some of my uncles teased me because I couldn't recognize them. Some said,

"We were so sad when we were told you had gone blind because we knew we had to start guiding you everywhere, thus reducing the chances of getting an in-law."

I just laughed because I now could afford to, but before I wouldn't have imagined that statement being funny.

During the service, which was conducted by Julius, a church elder, the message reflected on how God is able to do the impossible things in our lives. The message encouraged the congregation to have faith in God and always to depend on Him and not the superstitions that the world has. Mum then gave everyone a brief narration of the whole experience. I was smiling because I had told her before that she was going to have a great time retelling the story to everyone who came to visit.

After the service, the church choir sang the song which they had composed after I had gone blind. After the choir finished singing, I was asked to give a vote of thanks. At first I was fine as I thanked everyone for their prayers. I even cracked a joke. As I continued to talk, I was suddenly overcome with tears and I couldn't help myself crying. Dad told my aunt to take me back to my room. But then I told him, "Dad, I want to do this. I have to do this." Everyone was silent as they watched me dry my tears and recompose myself and continued to say,

"I thank God that today I am able to stand before all of you and actually see you, even though it is a bit blurred. I thank all of you for coming to witness God's miracle. I thank my parents and siblings for their love and support through this tough and rough uncertain experience. And for all my friends who gave me support through prayers, and time. I just want to thank you all and God bless you." I finished amid applause.

The choir continued singing throughout the afternoon. I went over and shook hands with everyone who had attended. I felt loved. My brothers, Evarist and Raphael who were absent, called and I updated them about my grand welcome party. Even though it was sad that they couldn't be there, I was glad that they were relieved and pleased that I was recovering.

The following days involved feasting and visits from friends and family. Like I had mentioned earlier, a child is of the community. The spirit of togetherness was evident throughout this period. Some people came to find out what was happening in our compound due to the numbers that came in and left through the gate. Others even thought there was a wedding since people who have just come from hospitalization are not normally welcomed in that manner. However, during weddings and funerals people show up in numbers in order to offer their support for the family. As usual Mum had to narrate the whole story to them. I even suggested to her to just record it on tape and just play it for the visitors. She just smiled and chased me away to my grandmothers. Whenever I walked on my own, sometimes I would trip over stools or whatever obstacle that was in my way. Mum told people to always clear my path. Whenever I wanted to sit, I would have to feel for the chair to make sure I didn't sit on a remote or whenever I wanted to go to the kitchen I had to feel for the door in order not to walk into it.

Lucky somehow found this amusing. Sometimes he would just sit and watch me struggle to look for my phone or my sandals. I wanted to be as independent as possible. So I never wanted him to help me unless I became frustrated and needed his help. In order not to struggle a lot looking for my things, I keep them in a specific place and in a certain order so as not to get confused. If anyone was to alter my arrangement, I would be frustrated as I searched for whatever thing, only to find it not far away from the original position.

Nonetheless I was glad to be back home. In the mornings, I would wake up just in time for the sunrise to witness the spectacular breaking of the dawn. The morning rays of the sun kissed my face as I stood watching it beyond the horizon of Lake Victoria. I had experienced my first brilliant sunrise in months. In the evenings, I went to the beach on the other side of town to watch the sun set. The moment the golden sun gently kissed the horizon of the lake as a gentle breeze swept over the water causing ripples, while birds soared towards their nests in preparation for the night; was breathtaking.

I finally saw the photo Ken had brought for me while I was at Hope Hospital. I looked at my chubby self and smiled. Then Dad told me how almost every night during my hospitalization, he had taken that photo and knelt down on the floor as he cried to God to save his little girl. He alternatingly looked at the photo then up at the sky as he implored the Creator of the universe to spare my life. It reminded me of the time Mum told me of how Dad broke down into tears on the day I had gone blind, as he spoke to his mother saying, "Mother, my daughter is blind. She cannot see!" I was teary just picturing him that broken and distraught. Having the strongest man I know cry to his mother like that made my heart sad and full of pity for my Dad. It was a situation which shook even the strongest of men and rendered them helpless.

On 4th May 2008, Mum, Lucky and I went to Nairobi, Kenya to take Lucky back to school. As we drove into the city that night, I was a bit disheartened as I looked at once the familiar places that were now blurred. We arrived at Aunt Nellie's house-she had been my guardian throughout my high school life, the moment she saw me, she broke down into tears. She embraced me for a long time as she cried, saying, "My daughter, you are back." She then started dancing as she shouted praises to God. Betsy, her daughter and my very good friend, also hugged me. We were really happy to see each other.

I spent the whole night narrating the story to Betsy as my Mum narrated it to Aunt Nellie. I showed Betsy all the photos of the friends I had made while in USA. It was a great night. No one wanted to go to bed. I also gave my other friends in Nairobi-Georgina, Charlene and Cynthia, a ring to let them know I was in town and really wanted to meet them.

The following day, I went to pick up my high school results which had been released while I was in hospital. As we drove into the school compound, I looked at the familiar place that I had spent the last four years in. It had not changed at all; the big roundabout filled with a selection of flowers just as one walks in was still there, and the chapel that stood out in the middle of the compound came into view. The six stone blocks of dormitories which housed the students stood in a semi-circle just as they had done for decades. The massive dining hall next to the parking lot was flocking with students having their tea break. I just smiled thinking that had been me a few months back.

Georgina and Charlene came to meet me there. We embraced for a long time as they shook my body and repeatedly asked me if I could actually see. They helped me up the stairs to the staffroom where I met my former teacher, Miss Tuimur. She was so glad that I was recovering. I also met Miss Karanja, my house matron, who had taken care of me in the dormitory. She is well advanced in age but has the flexibility of a young, agile person and was always very firm on her principles. She was so glad to see me and prayed that I would recover fully. All the other teachers that I met also showed their deepest concern for me and I was thankful that they had put me in their prayers. I also met some students who had been my juniors, who cried as they repeatedly asked me, "Maggie, are you okay? Can you see now?" they all asked with eagerness in their voices and showed a lot of concern. I just smiled and told them,

"I'm fine; I thank God that I can see your faces now."

"So, you were really blind? I mean completely?" one asked.

"Was it scary?" another followed.

"Are you going to recover your full sight?" another queried.

I just smiled and looked at them. The bell interrupted, signaling the end of their break and they all rushed off, as they looked back and waved, I waved back to them. I then knocked at the principal's office. She beckoned me in and as soon as she saw me, she stood up and stretched her hand to greet me. She asked how I was holding up and told me that the entire school had dedicated their morning services to pray for me. I was deeply touched by their gesture of concern. It felt good being back there. That evening, we had dinner at another family friend's house, Mrs. Pauline Kalonzo, also known as Mama Kevin. She had really been helpful in terms of taking care of Lucky while we were in the States. She gave a prayer of thanksgiving after Mum had narrated the whole ordeal.

5th, May 2008, we were supposed to head back to Musoma but we postponed the trip to the next day since Mum was slightly unwell. I then had more time to meet up with my friends Georgina, Charlene, Cynthia Kambuni and Esther Muthumbi. They were all fascinated by the whole experience as I narrated it to them. Even as I re-told the story, I still had doubts that I had actually gone through it. But the weak eyesight and the scars around my belly always jolted my memory.

Time flew by and soon it was time to return to the U.S.A for a further follow up from the doctors. They were all pleased that my progress was impressive. My body was responding well to the treatment. Dr. Julie later told my uncle one day when he had gone to pick up a document that we had been lucky that we had gone to the hospital when we did. She said,

"The blindness was a warning of the fatality of her condition. It would have been followed by paralysis and later in the worst scenario, death."

"What do you mean doctor?" he asked, completely shocked at this revelation.

"The headaches she had been experiencing before were a warning of the already damaged optic nerve. Since they had not been discovered earlier, the blindness followed, hence the treatment she received. However had this also not been attended to, the intracranial pressure would have caused a blockage in the arteries causing immediate death," she explained.

"I am glad we were saved from that ending. Thank you doctor once again." Uncle Peter concluded. He later informed Mum about what the doctor had said. She in turn told me and I thanked God even more. There I was depressed that I had gone blind, but God was once again warning me and preventing an unfortunate outcome. Who would have thought that blindness would actually be a blessing in disguise?

I had fewer headaches and my vision had significantly improved. The ophthalmologist was impressed. He prescribed glasses to improve my vision since I was already able to count fingers with my left eye and could also read. I was then scheduled to see the doctors after another six months. They even granted that I could attend school since most institutions cater for visually-impaired students. All this time there had been no talk of school. I also got a chance to meet some of the friends while I was there for the two weeks. They were also amazed at how quickly I was recovering. I could see their faces with less difficulty now. I was sure I was recovering.

Every passing day, I felt that my vision was slightly better than the day before, and every passing day I always thanked God for that. Once I got my glasses, the images were impressively sharper.

Some of the items I had struggled with before became clearer. I was becoming my old self again, only this time one eye was way weaker than the other. The doctor had said it was because it had been more affected with the pressure. I was more independent, I could walk on my own in familiar territory, but would require assistance in places I wasn't familiar with. Sometimes I wouldn't see a stone on the road, or missed a pothole and stumbled. I would just laugh at myself and say, "One day at a time." I would go for days without having a headache. I had almost forgotten how relieving that was. My once-darkened world full of immense pain and tears was clearing up. I could only thank God for that.

Part Five

I started thinking about university since I was already bored with sitting at home with nothing to do. I wasn't going to let my condition hold me back from achieving my ambitions. My brother, Evarist helped me with university applications. My parents told me I did not have to push myself. I could just wait for one year before joining the university. However, they added that in case I felt that I was ready to start that very year, it was all up to me and I had their support. I told them,

"If God was able to restore my sight, I'm sure He'll be able to make me pull through my Law degree."

Other people told me,

"Maggie, I think you should consider changing your career path since law involves so much reading and your eyes may not be able to handle the pressure."

I just smiled and said,

"Law is what I'm going to study and nothing else."

A few months later I received an unconditional offer letter from the University of Leeds, England, to join their International Foundation Year (IFY) and then later pursue my Law degree when I successfully excelled in my exams. I was so excited. Evarist had just graduated from the University of Bradford which is a few miles from Leeds. As I prepared to go Leeds, I asked God to provide people who would be willing to help me adjust and fit in to the society. I was excited about going to the university but at the same time, I was anxious about being in an alien place without my family and friends. I was so afraid since I wasn't sure how I was going to cope with my condition, which I was still adjusting to.

13th, September 2008, I arrived in Leeds with Mum. I looked around trying to familiarize myself with my new surroundings, since I knew this was going to be my home for the next four years. After we settled in that weekend, I couldn't wait for Monday so that I could visit the campus and begin the registration process. Mum helped me settle in, which was very helpful. The day she left,

I cried so much since she was the only person I had been talking to since we got to Leeds.

When I first walked onto the campus, everyone seemed to be in a rush and everything seemed to pass by so fast, as I struggled to find the different buildings within the university. It was so scary seeing all these people rush through the university, seeming to know where they were headed. I felt so alone and lost. Since I could not read the directions or signs clearly, I had a difficult time finding my way around. What was worse, after a week I had not even made a single friend! I was afraid to look people straight in the face without staring at them as I studied their faces. I found the Equality Service at the university, who deals with students with disabilities. They were very helpful. They showed me the different ways they would help me such as offering reading material in large print. By going to the centre, I somehow felt awkward since I had never needed these services before. Sometimes I didn't want to accept the fact that I was registered as visually impaired. Whenever I had these internal debates, I would finish off by saying, "Maggie, whether you accept it or not, you still need help and you cannot see properly, so it is up to you."

After giving myself the pep talk, I felt more confident. It was difficult at first to make new friends, mainly because I was afraid people wouldn't accept me the way I am. The first few friends I made were my fellow foundation year students, because whenever we were told to read an article which was in small print, whoever sat next to me was asked to read for me by our tutor, Tom.

After registering with the GP at Leeds Student medical Practice, I had to give them my medical records. They organized for me to meet with a neurosurgeon and ophthalmologist so that they could monitor my condition. After a session with the ophthalmologist, he registered me as blind and referred me to the Social Services who paid me a couple of visits. They offered various gadgets to help me cope with my disability. Since I had gone past the denial stage, it was easy for them to give me the equipment, for example the magnifiers to help me with my reading. They even asked me whether I needed an assistant to help me move around from my accommodation to the university and even around the city centre. I told them it wouldn't be necessary since I would try finding my own way. Whenever I missed a step and stumble on the side of the road or bump into fellow pedestrians or hit a post, I wished I had an assistant. But then again I dismiss the idea.

In November 2008, Raphael came to visit me as he had not seen me since January, when I was still critically ill. He was so surprised to see how I was able to do so many things on my own. He couldn't believe it when I went to pick him up from the bus station on my own. I even gave him a mini tour of Leeds. He was finally convinced that I was fine since he had not believed it whenever he was told that I was doing well on my own. For the last image he had had was of me crying in my own darkness as we took a walk round the hospital. I had been told how stressed he had been in the months that followed and didn't want anybody mentioning about me being sick. His friends also wished for my quick recovery as they hated seeing Raphael depressed and disoriented from his usual self.

God answered my prayers. I have made friends who accept me the way I am. Sometimes even as we walk through the city centre or the university, they warn me whenever they see that I am about to hit a pole or walk into someone or into a puddle of water. When we go to watch a movie, they hold my hand as we get inside the dark cinema.

My course mates, Hamad and Farhan, helped me with my reading and mobility round campus. Trish and Hira were very helpful with the social activities like shopping, movies and even cooking. They are very understanding and patient. Hira also makes sure that people don't leave things lying around the house so that I don't trip on them. She also helps me find the different hospitals where I am to attend clinics. She is a selfless person who goes the extra mile to make sure I cope well with my condition. For this I am forever grateful. I also befriended Tanveer after we both had lost sight of our tour guide and discovered we were both visually impaired. It was comforting to know that someone else understood exactly how I felt. There was also Mark, who lived in the same place as I did. He also helped me know my way around Leeds as he had been there longer than I. These six were the first people who knew about my condition and have helped me ever since. I really thank God, for He answered that prayer.

I successfully completed my foundation course and got accepted into Law School. I have made more friends who, as the days go by, get to learn about my extraordinary experience. I thank God that I was able to go through this whole experience and live to tell the tale. I still encounter obstacles some days since my vision is not perfect. However, I am glad that I am studying the course I have always wished to study.

Life is a challenge. It can throw so many things at you, and at the end of the day it depends on how you receive whatever life throws at you. To say the least, I have been through the pit and out. I have a condition that I have to live with for the rest of my life. Each day I am not sure what to expect, so I always leave it to God for He knows what lies ahead. There are many challenges ahead, but every time I look back at the year 2008, I know I can face whatever may come my way, for I have been through a journey of darkness, and am ready to face the ongoing journey with it's challenges.

From this whole experience I have learnt to trust in God more. He saw me through it all. He never left my side even once. So many people go through difficult and trying experiences and lose hope. I want everyone who hears about this story to praise God. Some may not be believers in the existence of God, but I have good news for you. There is still time and God is waiting for you. Friends, family, doctors may fail you sometimes but God is always there. I was lucky that my parents could afford my treatment. Had it been otherwise, maybe today there would be no story to tell. Many people back home go through this every day but they have no one to shed a light on their situation, and hence go through life having lost all hope. I pray that more cases of blindness are looked into so that if there is a chance of saving a life then it is done. I implore thee dear reader to tell of this incredible story to all and sundry.

"And we know that all things work together for the good of those who love God, to those who are called according to his purpose." Romans 8:28

Amen.

Epilogue

Four years on and I am still going strong. Looking back at these past years I am amazed at how quickly time has elapsed. It was just yesterday when I first ventured into the unfamiliar territory of university life at the University of Leeds and now in a few months I will be graduating, leaving this prestigious institution, but I know the great times will follow me for life. It almost seems too unreal. I have grown in more ways than one, made great lifetime friends, interacted with other people with disabilities and challenged myself to beat the odds every time. I look back in awe and smile for I know that the future is still bright and no matter what obstacles may come my way, I can take them on with confidence and pride.

I was slightly lost in my first year in University as a International Foundation student trying to fit in to a new learning environment in a foreign country while still adjusting to being partially-sighted. Most freshmen at university are usually trying to find their way anyway, but I had to go an extra mile. Knowing me now, some might say it's hard to believe but I was shy, reserved and afraid to look people in the eye because I didn't want them to feel like I was staring at them. I was always cautious and even paranoid sometimes thinking that these people could see that I was struggling. All these new faces, students rushing up and down the campus with confidence and at ease as they chatted and chuckled in lectures, cafes or in the library. It was not until I went to the Global Cafe, an event organised for International students to help them find fellow students from the four corners of the world, that I made my first friends. I had gone there with Joe, a former schoolmate of my brother Raphael. He had also just arrived in Leeds and didn't know that many people. I was wearing a bandana with the Tanzanian flag when someone tapped my shoulder and asked if that is where I was from. I told her I was and she introduced herself as Trish, and said she was from Kenya. She had come with a couple of new friends she had made who lived in the same accommodation as her and studied the same course. One of them was Hira, a shy and reserved girl from Pakistan. We didn't talk much that night but I exchanged contacts with all of them and promised to keep in touch.

Days flew by. I met up with Trish and Hira a couple of times for coffee, a movie or dinner. Fearing how they would react, I was at first reluctant to tell them about my condition. As I got to know them, I became more comfortable and eventually told them and to my relief, they were understanding and supportive. They would always be on the look out for me as we walked through the campus or in the city centre. We weren't in the same course so we had to try to fit in or lunch breaks and coffees when it suited all of us best. I reminisce about the chats and laughs we had, talking about our families back home, sometimes even skyping or talking with each others' families. Trish is charismatic, smart, funny. She is always updated on the happenings of the world. We went to rival high schools so this dominated our conversations quite a lot. Sometimes we would be so deep into discussing mutual friends from back in Nairobi that we would forget Hira had no clue of what we were talking about. We would apologise and resume talking about the courses and assignments or upcoming events in the Union.

At first, Hira appeared to be the quiet one, the one who would only smile and not comment much. With time she would contribute and talk just as loud and when I commented about this she said, "Maggy, you are so loud if I don't shout you won't hear me!" She has long flowing jet black hair that contrasts perfectly with her radiant, fair skin. Her eyes are so bright and beautiful and always groomed with care and they sparkle every time she blinks. I always tell her she would make a perfect eye model. She is a true confidant, an easy person to talk to, funny, so smart (she got almost a full scholarship for being one of the top students in her A-level and later acquired a full-year work placement in Morgan Stanley, one of the leading investment banks). She is genuinely caring, supportive, loving and humble. As I got to know her over the past four years, every day I am thankful for having her in my life. Dad met her that December after we had come back from the US for my check up. Hira hadn't gone home for Christmas and neither had I. After just spending a few hours with her, he advised me to keep her as a close friend for she appeared to be a good person. I have never doubted those words.

By this time I had made another friend from my course-Hamad, from Qatar. I didn't speak much to him at first since he already seemed to have made friends of his own among our course mates. A confident boy with a charming baby face. He has a great sense of humour, which I instantly liked since I was always cracking up at his jokes and comments in class. One day he just asked me,

"You do laugh quite a lot in class."

"Well you are funny," I replied, restraining a chuckle.

"Really? Thanks. You always seem to get my jokes. I can see we are going to be great friends. I make the jokes, you laugh, we complement each other!" he replied, smiling, revealing his dimples.

"Sounds good to me," I remarked.

The next time I saw him I was showing my high school friend, Sheila, round campus as she was visiting from Bradford where she studied. I introduced them and instantly Hamad offered to help. I was so relieved since I hadn't been to most areas around campus myself. Next thing you know, Sheila and I are bursting out in laughter at Hamad's jokes. I later introduced Hamad to Trish and Hira and they all immediately bonded. That was the beginning of a beautiful friendship. They all treated me as equal, helped me where I needed help and I did the same. Since I did not want to burden anyone with questions all the time, I would spend my free time finding my way around campus or the city centre on my own. It came in handy when we all needed to find a certain place and I would always know where it was well most of the time at least.

Another friend whom I made while in foundation was Farhan, from Malaysia. I remember one of the first things I said to him as we waited to go into class was,

"You smile a lot!"

"Pretty much," was all he said, brandishing a huge smile and revealing his sparkling white teeth.

I mostly saw Farhan in class, since we had all the same classes. We would help each other study, which was very helpful. He is an eloquent, ambitious and very confident person who always seems to have an answer to every argument, whether relevant or not. He has impeccable taste in fashion and also in great cuisine.

Together with his aspirations in politics, he has always wanted to be a prominent lawyer just like his father he always carries himself in distinguished manner.

I also met Shafiq who was studying the same course as Trish and Hira. He always smiled, was quiet but a keen listener and very humble. These (and a few others) are the only people who knew about my condition, I did not even tell my housemates, whom I lived with for one year. I made sure I carried out my household chores well so that no one suspected anything or asked questions, and they didn't. My first year in Leeds just flew by. I had settled in well, made new friends and adjusted to my circumstances. I handled my studies well and successfully excelled in my exams, which granted me a partial scholarship for my three year pursuit of my law degree.

The next three years just flew by. I made more friends. There was Omair, Hira's brother, who joined the university the following year. We immediately bonded since we were all living together, including my brother Evarist who by this time was taking his Masters at Leeds University. Unlike his sister, he was not shy or reserved but rather outspoken, knowledgeable, always taking pleasure in making fun of Hira and I, just because he could. I always tell him he reminds me of my brother Lucky, who enjoys treating me like his little sister even though I am older. Sometimes he and Hira would accompany me to my medical check-ups, hold my hand when crossing the street and also remove all obstacles blocking my path. Before Omair knew just how bad my eyesight was, he would always blame me for ignoring him as he waved at me on campus. I just told him, "If you are not standing right in front of me chances are I won't see you!" It was great having all of them in that house. Our initials spelled HOME (Hira, Omair, Maggy, Evarist) and that is what it was, a home of loving, caring individuals whom you could depend on for anything. So many cherished memories, family dinners, birthdays, and game nights filled with music, dance and laughter.

I also met Azy from Malaysia as well. She is so full of life. She instantly makes friends with just about anyone she meets. She is a great friend, highly spirited, fun and funny, determined and always showing great concern for others. Through her I met more people-Kristina, Carmen, Mandie and Carol. My family in Leeds continued to grow. Azy introduced me to the Malaysian society and I fitted right in. I even directed a play for them and was also the host. I had always had a passion for drama and since my ordeal I had not taken part in any production. This was a great opportunity to learn about a different culture. I even dragged Farhan in to take part in the play and be my co-host since ironically I was in the society and he wasn't! This also gave me the opportunity for public speaking-something I was also quite good at back in high school but had not practised since I joined Leeds. At first I was afraid that I would mess up or humiliate myself. However, once I saw all the support I received from my friends who had come to watch, I took a deep breath and took to the stage and entertained my audience through the evening. The roars of laughter and applauds steered me on and the fear completely subsided.

Later that year, Richard Mbasu, a final year student from Kenya, initiated the East African Society. He asked me to be co-vice president together with Chris Muthamia, also from Kenya, as well as Sharifa, who was the Public Relations Officer. We held our first event, which showed potential for the growth of the society since there was quite a large East African Community at the university. It was a forum for students to meet their fellow citizens as well as reflect on life back home. At the end of that year Richard graduated and since the society was still in its budding stage, he asked me to step in and be president. I was reluctant at first since I was not sure I would be fit to take up this great responsibility. For me it meant explaining to more people why I didn't see them when they waved at me on campus, or why I couldn't see their raised hands when in a discussion. I spoke to my parents about this since I was at home for summer when it happened. They were very understanding and also encouraged me to face my fears since people would understand if I explained to them my condition. I took up the position and with a team of dedicated committee members, we made quite a big name for our society. We held a series of events- socials, parties, dinners and charity fundraisers such as the Tribal Instinct fashion show held in March 2011. It attracted a rich variety of people due to our cosmopolitan selection of models. The funds raised were used to build a classroom and a kitchen for the orphans of Ketwang'i in Kisumu, Kenya.

It was during this period of working for the society that Sharifa and I got close. We started off as just colleagues but eventually became great friends. We would work on the very minute details of these events, and though frustrated at times, we would still carry on to make sure the society ran smoothly. The society dominated most of our conversations and we would spend all our free time getting in contact with different organisations and people who would help our society. Sharifa is a hardworking, self-driven, dependable, creative person who is not only great to work with but also a true friend and great companion. She is always available both for emotional and physical support.

In conjunction with being the society president, I was also working in the University supermarket as a part-time retail assistant. At first, it was confusing and intimidating serving at the till. I would take almost twice as long to scan the items as my fellow colleagues. I did not give up and with time I could serve just as fast as the rest. There are minor set backs from time to time but these do not hold me back. I was able to juggle school work, society commitments and my job, something which I had not anticipated when I first joined the university. Most of the people I worked with still don't know I am visually impaired.

At last now I am in my final year. In a few months I will be graduating. I still work at the shop. I am no longer the president of the East African Society but I'm now the Culture Representative at the Student Union in charge of over thirty different societies. My main aim is to help the students fit right into the Leeds Community. It can be quite daunting and lonely being in a new place, but if you have people from your country they can reduce the pangs of being homesick. I also interact with a number of disabled students who are constantly battling any setbacks their conditions may put forth. I am always encouraged every time I hear their inspiring experiences.

Nonetheless, what started out as a scary embrace of the unknown has turned out to be a life-changing experience. Most days I go without thinking about my eyes. I live my life to the fullest. However, some days I become emotional when I am desperately trying to read a notice at a distance, or a sign across the road, or watch a plane fly across the sky-I can hear it but cannot see it; or when I walk into something-a bin, electric post, a door! Or when I trip on the curb, when someone is stretching out their hand in greeting and I don't realise until someone mentions it later and I am embarrassed. I could go on and on but why dwell on the negative while the positive is overwhelming? I can see the faces of my family and friends; I am able to study and handle pressure from the course. I work, take part in social events, can witness the sunset and behold the full moon. I can live independently-cook, clean, shop own my own. I tell people my story and they are inspired. I have so much to be grateful for that it would be a crime not to appreciate it. I urge you never to let life's challenges prevent you from achieving your full potential.

And so my journey continues...